Praise

"Mark was born with a traveler's eye, one that sees below the surface, and a writer's voice, to share what he sees in ways that enlighten others."
ARNIE WEISSMANN, EDITOR IN CHIEF, *TRAVEL WEEKLY*

"Pour yourself a drink, fasten your seatbelt, and get ready for the trip of a lifetime. *Prepare for Departure* is a book filled with laughter and poignant experiences that will inspire you to pursue your dreams and appreciate life to the fullest. Above all, it's about unconditional love, and the special bond shared between a son and his mother."
ROBERT ADAMS, EDITORIAL DIRECTOR, *PASSPORT MAGAZINE*

"In this memoir for today, travel writer and self-confessed aviation nerd Mark Chesnut presents a different kind of guidebook. With writing that is often achingly beautiful, weirdly hilarious and always brutally honest, Chesnut shares his family's history over the course of decades, all while interweaving stories from his successful career traveling the world. Ultimately, the journey along this road arrives at a greater acceptance of the fragility of life, and the faults and courage that make us human."
KENNETH SHAPIRO, PUBLISHER/EDITOR-IN-CHIEF, *TRAVELAGE WEST*

"Packed with tight, elegant prose, Mark Chesnut's charming memoir explores a childhood, youth, and travel writing career through the prism of his mother's caring, her eccentric rules, her fears for his future as a gay man, her parade of quirky relatives, and mostly through the lens of her final years in nursing homes. This is a story of a child who preferred designing his own airline to doing homework, and who understood that hotels and traveling could lead to adventures, passions and contentment. It is a story of unashamed love, and ̶̶̶̶̶̶̶̶̶̶̶̶̶̶̶̶̶̶̶̶̶̶̶̶̶̶̶ ̶avel that results in both success an ̶̶̶̶̶̶̶̶̶̶̶̶̶̶̶̶̶̶̶̶̶̶̶̶̶̶ l enjoy the ride: its wit, its candor, its ̶̶̶̶̶̶̶̶̶̶̶̶̶̶̶̶̶̶̶̶̶̶̶̶̶̶ now I did."
GEOFFREY WEILL,
ALL ABROAD, A M̶̶̶̶̶̶̶̶̶̶̶̶̶̶̶̶̶̶̶̶̶̶

"A warm-hearted, funny memoir about growing up different. Yes, he works as a travel writer, but Mark Chesnut reminds us that life itself is a journey, with our family as our constant traveling companions. Mark's delightful voyage with his irrepressible mother, Eunice, is poignant, humorous, and deeply moving. With its vivid characters, awkward life lessons, and valuable travel tips, *Prepare for Departure* is filled with trials, triumphs, and laughter. It's a trip you won't want to miss. Buckle up! It's going to be a bumpy—but also extremely entertaining—ride!"
ANN LESCHANDER, WRITER/DIRECTOR, *THE PARK BENCH*

"Like David Sedaris, Chesnut weaves dark humor (as well as a healthy dose of 1970s nostalgia) into his clever prose as he describes his misfit childhood, eccentric relatives and his mother's emotional final months. Tears may be shed, but they're never far removed from the next chuckle that this book will surely elicit. We may not fully understand Chesnut's fantastic obsession with all things travel; not many authors, after all, have pretended to be a flight attendant on an abandoned school bus or stolen departure signs from airports. But we can all relate to his universal themes of love, loss, laughter and forgiveness."
LISA TAKEUCHI CULLEN, AUTHOR,
REMEMBER ME: A LIVELY TOUR OF THE AMERICAN WAY OF DEATH

"With pathos and aplomb, travel writer Mark Chesnut's enchanting book gathers essays about his aging mother and growing up in the 1970s as part of a single-parent household. Warm and elegiac, the memoir voices a son's love for his inimitable mother."
FOREWORD REVIEWS

About the Author

Mark Chesnut is a New York City-based journalist, editor and public speaker with more than twenty years of experience. The 2019 winner of the NLGJA Excellence in Travel Writing Award, Mark has written for Fodor's, *Forbes Travel Guide*, *HuffPost*, the *Miami Herald*, *Travel+Leisure Mexico*, the New York Times bestseller *1,000 Places To See Before You Die* and the in-flight magazines of *Aeromexico*, *American Airlines*, and *Avianca*. He writes about Latin America in his travel blog, LatinFlyer.com, and contributes regularly to travel industry media outlets including *Travel Weekly*, *TravelAge West*, *TravelPulse* and meeting industry publications including *Successful Meetings* and *Meetings & Conventions Magazine*. He also speaks at a variety of travel industry and publishing events.

When flying, Mark prefers an aisle seat, unless you're able to give him an upgrade, in which case he'll sit anywhere you tell him to.

MarkChesnut.com

Prepare for Departure

Mark Chesnut

www.vineleavespress.com

A catalogue record for this book is available from the National Library of Australia

For Eunice Clayton Chesnut, who gave me the travel bug and always made sure I had a typewriter.

Author's Note

This book is a memoir and a work of creative nonfiction. It reflects the author's present recollections of experiences over time. Some events have been compressed or combined, some dialogue has been recreated and some names, locations, and characteristics have been modified to protect the privacy of the people and organizations involved and to provide you with a more interesting trip.

Preboarding

(that's what you call a prologue
when you're a travel addict)

The flight attendant, stylishly garbed in a forest green wrap dress and seafoam scarf, could barely conceal her excitement as she climbed the circular stairway. Relaxing upstairs, in the luxuriously carpeted second-floor lounge of the Chesway Global 747, was one of the hottest new musical groups of the 1970s, fully decked out in rhinestones, matching jeans, and gigantic sunglasses. It was up to the flight attendant to advise these beloved music makers when the aircraft reached a comfortable cruising altitude, at which point they'd descend to the first-class cabin and make history as the first top-forty group ever to perform live on a scheduled commercial flight.

This momentous event was the brainchild of none other than Mark Chesnut, founder and CEO of Chesway Global, one of the world's fastest-growing airlines in the late 1970s. Chesnut, a native of Brockport, New York, overcame his small-town beginnings—and the kids who made fun of him—to become one of the coolest and most talked-about airline executives in the industry, garnering rave reviews for attention-getting gimmicks like in-flight musical performances and the world's first dancing flight attendants. He now lives in a luxurious penthouse apartment in—

"Mark!"

"What Mom?" I rolled my eyes and looked up from the sketchpad spread out on the red shag rug in my bedroom. She leaned against my bedroom door, one hand on her hip.

"Did you finish your homework?"

"I'm working on my airline," I whined. "Can you please just leave me alone for a while?"

"You can go back to drawing after you finish your homework." She sighed. "You're never going to start an airline if you flunk seventh grade."

10

1. The Last Road Trip

My mother arrived in New York City with a black eye and one arm dangling in a sling.

By the time the dirty white van finally swerved to a halt after seven hours navigating the highways of New York State, I'd been waiting on the street for more than an hour. The truck looked like something that kidnappers might drive. The sign on its side—a cheap magnetic logo that identified the vehicle as a non-emergency medical transportation vehicle—seemed like a perfect ruse for spiriting away some wealthy heiress to a remote cabin in the woods to await a ransom.

The driver jumped out and opened the back door, but there was no sumptuously garbed kidnapping victim inside. It was just my eighty-nine-year-old mother, strapped into a wheelchair tethered to the wall of the otherwise gapingly empty van.

"I thought that trip was never going to end," she blurted as the lift lowered her wheelchair onto the steamy sidewalk in front of the Venerable Hills Care and Rehabilitation Center. I hadn't seen her in nearly three weeks, but she offered no smile, no kiss hello. I kneeled and wrapped my arm around her bony frame as I kissed her forehead.

With her matted gray hair, limp right arm, and right eye ringed by oversized bruises, Eunice Chesnut looked like an

11

ancient soldier returning from war. But my mother's injuries weren't combat-related; they were the result of her latest fall at the assisted living facility where she'd lived for just over a year in upstate New York.

Now, here she was, frowning at the sidewalk and examining her veiny hands. She didn't cast even the briefest of glances at the imposing brick-and-glass building that towered in front of her.

Did she understand she'd be living here in New York City now? Did she remember selling her own home a couple of years earlier? Or retiring from her job at age eighty-eight, selling her car, and moving into assisted living?

"Well, so what are we going to do now, sweetie?" she asked, squinting into the sunlight as she smoothed her wrinkled blouse with her good hand.

Thanks to an extensive round of tests at a sprawling hospital on the outskirts of Rochester, we knew why my mother had become so confused and unbalanced in recent months. A large brain tumor had taken up residence inside her skull. When she'd gotten the news just a few weeks earlier, she'd called me from the hospital and declared that she would not seek treatment.

"I am *old,* and I don't want them to do *anything* to me," she had said, her voice weak but resolute. "There's no point in putting myself through some awful surgery or any more suffering when I might only live another year or two. I've already had a very good life. But when it's time to go, it's time to go, kiddo."

After the fall and the diagnosis, the assisted living facility in her town couldn't meet her needs anymore. Neither could I nor my sister Glynn, since we lived in New York City and New Jersey and worked full time. So, after several days of research, I called my mother at the hospital to talk about her moving somewhere new—and I made sure to not call the new place what it really was: a *nursing home.*

"Momma, Glynn and I have found a really nice place for you to live, near where I live in New York City, so we can see each other all the time," I said as brightly as I could. "Would you like that?"

"That sounds wonderful, sweetie." She was almost always cheerful, even in the hospital. While her decades living in the Great Lakes region may have imbued her voice with a decidedly Midwestern tone, her Southern-born manners dictated the content of what came out of her mouth. That meant she remained upbeat and polite whenever possible.

The urgency of Eunice's move to the Big Apple had thrown a monkey wrench into the Hollywood-style plans that I had previously concocted. I had wanted to fly up to Rochester to accompany her on the long ride down to the city. I had imagined a meaningful trip laden with emotional discovery and reconciliation, like something you'd see in some sappy TV movie. I'd be the doting son with a constant smile that illuminated the interior of the handsomely appointed black luxury SUV that would have surely been our form of transportation. We'd reminisce about all the vacations we'd taken together. Ponder how she gave me the travel bug and the tools to become a travel writer. Reflect on the symbolism of what would likely have been our final road trip together. Maybe we'd even discuss weighty issues like why I had to cancel my wedding plans because of her. Or why she hid the only published book I'd ever written. So much to discuss! And so appropriate for the emotional bonding to take place as we charged down the New York State Thruway, the thoroughfare that had once served as a gateway for our long-distance adventures.

As we reviewed and resolved every possible aspect of our mother-son relationship during that final trip, heartfelt soundtrack music would swell as the driver finally opened the vehicle's perfectly polished door to welcome us to the glistening high-rise nursing home where Eunice would spend the last days of her life. My mother and I would be emotionally renewed and fortified, ready to confidently face her impending decline with Oscar-worthy strength, an even stronger mother-son bond, and a well-honed sense of humor. Cue the music again as we enter the facility, hand in hand. And cut.

But there was no time for that soul-strengthening voyage. My mother's latest fall and diagnosis had accelerated the need for her to move downstate, and I had to stay in New York City to hastily arrange her accommodations at the nursing home. A couple of her wonderful, always-supportive friends saw her off, but she traveled on her own, bandaged up in a wheelchair, in the back of that empty white van. The cathartic moments would have to take place here, at the nursing home—although I now realized that I'd probably be journeying down memory lane by myself as her awareness continued to fade.

My mother was exhausted and confused, but sure of one thing as the nursing home's glass doors slid open with an air-conditioned whoosh: she was ready to leave this Earth.

2. The Three Stages of Grief

(at least for me, a long time ago)

I wasn't sure how I'd deal with my mother's looming demise, but I was positive it would be a far cry from how I reacted to my father's death more than forty years earlier.

You might have heard of the five stages of grief described by psychiatrist Elisabeth Kübler-Ross in her book *On Death and Dying*: denial, anger, bargaining, depression, and acceptance. I, however, experienced grief about my father's death with a more streamlined, efficient, and far-more-entertaining *three* stages.

Also, my stages have much more interesting names: prancing, pooping, and partridges.

I guess I should explain.

Stage 1: Prancing

"My daddy's dead! My daddy's dead!" I shouted gleefully whenever anyone visited our home during one rather dramatic week in January 1969.

I actually don't remember cheerily proclaiming my father's passing as I pranced up and down the blue carpeted steps of our split-level home in Brockport, New York. My mother told me that I did.

"You were only four years old, and you didn't understand what was going on," she explained years later. "For you, your father dying just meant you were getting more attention from the grownups."

I can imagine what we must have looked like back then. My mother would have been neatly tucked into a long, poly-cotton blend skirt and matching blouse, or possibly a knit dress, maybe a pleasant light gray or baby blue color, her ample figure tamed by a girdle and her dark, wavy hair combed into near submission. I was probably wearing an overly soft post-toddler T-shirt decorated with the sewn-on image of a train or a car, my bright orange hair dancing like flames as I skipped merrily (okay, gaily) across the low-cut carpeting.

Daddy's death was certainly a great chance for me to shine for visitors. But I apparently misinterpreted my assigned role. Instead of portraying the grieving, doe-eyed young son, I opted for the dazzle of a hyperactive kid who'd probably been sipping too much of his mother's heavily caffeinated soda pop. Family friends who came to call must have smiled uncomfortably, silently wishing they could gently shove me into the coat closet as I ran circles around the modern Danish furniture, milking our family's loss to the max.

Stage 2: Pooping

I guess you could say that taking a crap in public was a misguided attempt at acceptance. But I'm considering it part of the grieving process since death can throw surviving family members into situations that require new strategies for survival. And some of them might be smelly.

John J. Chesnut, Jr. died of lung cancer at age fifty-one, in the same hospital where I was born in Brockport. My father's death placed my mother, for the first time in her life, squarely in the driver's seat. What had been a traditional, four-person family suddenly became a single-parent household. And it shrank even more within a matter of months, when my older sister, Glynn, graduated from high school and went away to college, just as I was about to start kindergarten. (I was one of those surprise babies born late in the family timeline, but that's another story.)

My mother decided that we didn't need a big house anymore, so she rented out our red split-level to another family and moved the two of us to an apartment complex near the Erie Canal with stately white columns and a verdant shared courtyard that belied the fact this development was designed for people on a tight budget.

I started school as my mother began her studies at the State University of New York's College at Brockport. More than twenty years had passed since she had dropped out of the University of Louisville to get married and now, in her mid-forties, she decided to finally get her bachelor's degree. She chose history as a major rather than her first choice, English, because she didn't want to receive favored treatment just because her late husband had taught in that department.

With her college classes and a part-time secretarial job—not to mention volunteer work and an active social life—my mother was busy. Piles of books, magazines, and notebooks covered her tiny single bed, which seemed designed to assure potential suitors that she was not interested in dating. We visited the town library as much as we did the supermarket.

Suddenly finding myself an only child (at least the only one living at home) and with only one parent, I had plenty of free time to meet our new neighbors. I started tagging along with a bunch of slightly older kids—if I was five years old, they were probably seven or eight; tall, gangly white boys with freckles, military-style buzz cuts, and mothers who yelled commands from apartment windows like "get back in here before I smack you." Some of their fathers worked at Eastman Kodak, which at the time was the biggest employer in Rochester, just a few miles away.

One day, I followed the kids into the densely wooded lot next to our apartment complex. The biggest boy turned around and fixed his gaze on me.

"Why are you followin' us?" he asked. "You wanna be part of our group?" he asked.

"Yes!" I nodded excitedly at the possibility of being truly accepted by the big boys.

"Well then you've gotta do something."

I shifted uncomfortably in my little cowboy boots. "Ummm ... what do I have to do?"

The kid looked around the woods and then at his friends. He smiled. "You need to take a shit, right here."

"Really?"

"Yeah."

"But I don't have any toilet paper."

"Use leaves."

I didn't know if they'd made other kids poop in the woods as an initiation rite. And I didn't know if I'd be subjecting myself to humiliation by accepting the challenge. All I knew was that I wanted to be liked, and taking a dump certainly wasn't the worst price to pay for acceptance. So I agreed. The kids giggled as they walked down the trail to wait for me. I lowered my corduroys and baby blue underwear and squatted, distracting myself by inhaling the strange aroma that results from mixing forest leaves with human excrement.

That was the first time I remember purposely not telling my mother about something that I'd done. But my foray into the fecal forest was worth it. I got to hang out more with those boys. We played games like tag and red light/green light in the courtyard. Sometimes, my mother would fill a blue-and-white metal bucket with candy and lower it on a string from our balcony so that all the kids could pick a treat. Thanks to the candy and my increased street cred from the public pooping, I was a fairly popular kid at the apartment complex.

Stage 3: Partridges

After a couple years of apartment living, my mother decided that the space was too small. We moved back to our big red house on Fourth Section Road, an upgrade made possible through a combination of my father's life insurance, veteran's pension, and social security, supplemented by income from my mother's part-time secretarial job.

This was going to be fun. Not only did we get to go back to the big house, Mommy let me move into my sister's old room, which was bigger than the one I had before. To get me settled into my new digs, she went to the Big N discount department store to buy me a tiny black-and-white TV, which I excitedly placed on top of the fake wood entertainment console that she'd also bought for me. Finally, I could watch my favorite shows in the comfort of my own room.

The cathode rays beaming conveniently close to my bed became a constant source of reference as I became more aware of the world outside. I soon realized there weren't many people on TV who lived like I did. In the 1970s, the media provided very few images of single-parent households, and even fewer with only one kid. I loved *The Brady Bunch*, but that sitcom didn't represent my life. *The Courtship of Eddie's Father* didn't either, probably because it focused more on the parent than the kid, and there was no mother on the scene. A bit more relatable was *Julia*, Dianne Carroll's TV sitcom that ran from 1968 to 1971, which depicted the life of a single nurse and her precocious son.

For me, however, the media's most accurate depiction of a mother-son relationship like mine was *Alice Doesn't Live Here Anymore*, the 1974 Martin Scorsese film that won Ellen Burstyn an Academy Award for her portrayal of a frazzled widow with a bratty son named Tommy. The biggest difference between their situation and ours was that while job hunting, dating, and a fledgling singing career distracted Alice the most, my mother focused on studying, working, volunteer activities, and socializing with friends. But they did travel together like we did; Alice and Tommy embarked on a long road trip that reminded me of the ones we took multiple times every year, although the destinations were different, and my mother wasn't as viciously clever with her comebacks when I acted like a jerk.

For all the snarky realism that Alice provided, my greatest TV love during that time was *The Partridge Family*, the 1970 to 1974 sitcom that showcased the adventures of a musical family who, after the father's death, toured the country in a colorfully painted school bus, enchanting audiences and learning valuable lessons as they bickered jovially and sang their hearts out in plush velour costumes. I had all their records, and I did my best to drop the needle on my record player right when they started singing on TV, so the sound would synch perfectly. When I got the timing right, the confluence of sound was like having the musical group right there in the room with me.

I even wrote a letter to the Partridges. Actually, I dictated the letter to my overly patient mother, confident that her grown-up handwriting would impress Shirley and her son Keith, who were my two favorite characters.

"You are my favorite family," I gushed. "I hope some time you could come to Brockport, New York and make a show here. If you want to, you may come to our house. You may come in your bus or car. I would like it very much if you come in your bus. But do not come on a school day."

• • •

Okay, so maybe my three stages were a bit of a stretch. But the issues I dealt with—and my reactions to each—were directly related to my father's death.

Maybe it was easier for me as a young child to deal with death because I didn't have many recollections of my father. Some people claim to recall vast details from early childhood, but I don't. Most of my supposed memories about Daddy were the result of stories repeated by family members. Only a few must really be mine because they were too specific and inconsequential for anyone to have bothered mentioning to me later—unimportant little details like the dial-style handle on the water fountain near my father's office at the college, where he'd lift me up for a drink after he finished teaching English literature classes (most water fountains had a button, not a handle, so that machine fascinated me).

I also remember my father sitting lankily in a blue-striped chair in our family room, a beer in his hand, smiling and trying to grab me as I ran past, giggling. He didn't get up to chase me because he was already sick.

A few details about the hospital also stay in my mind from the weeks leading up to his death. But those memories aren't greeting-card-worthy images of precious final hours with Daddy. As his condition worsened, someone—I'm not sure whether it was a family member or the hospital staff—decided that I shouldn't visit him anymore in his hospital room. So I'd wait with a grownup in the sparkling clean cafeteria, a spectacular place filled with whirring machines designed to satisfy the high-tech gastronomic whims of exhausted friends and family members. One of the vending machines was especially eye-catching—a carousel-like affair with clear plastic doors that slid open to reveal an array of tasty, slightly chilled sandwiches. It was like something from a space station, and it was just about the most amazing thing I'd ever seen.

As I sat in the cafeteria with various family friends, I always knew that, eventually, Mommy's smiling face would appear beneath the bright fluorescent lights. Her short hair would be neatly combed into brown waves and—most importantly, as far as I was concerned—her gloved hands would be carrying gifts for me that Daddy had sent from his hospital room: plastic-wrapped eating utensils, complete with neatly folded napkins and tiny salt and pepper packets that you could sprinkle on whatever you wanted. Those were better than any store-bought present because they were things that real grown-ups used when they went someplace special, like a restaurant at an airport or a hospital.

One day, Mommy walked into the cafeteria and set a different kind of gift on the table in front of me: a giant clothespin, like the big old ones in our basement that she didn't even use anymore. Someone had painted a red and black uniform and a little face on this one, so it looked like a toy soldier. I didn't like the soldier as much as the pre-wrapped dining utensils—you can't eat imaginary food or pretend you're in a restaurant with a painted piece of wood, after all. Looking back now, I'm pretty sure that my father hadn't really sent me those gifts. My mother had most likely chosen them for me. Either way, I liked the little soldier and loved the utensils, and I was pretty much oblivious to the fact that, just down the hall, my father was dying.

• • •

Maybe I'm being self-centered by assuming that others would go through anything like my childhood grieving process. My mother, for example, took a decidedly practical approach to my father's death.

I don't remember her crying or mourning. She always looked the same, with her minimal makeup and low-maintenance haircut that required no beauty salon visits. Her wardrobe didn't get darker; she sported the same array of sometimes-colorful polyester pants and tops accompanied by practical shoes. She did, perhaps, add a few more pounds to the weight she had already failed to lose after my birth. There was no time for exercise as she busied herself with making decisions about the next steps our lives would take.

Uncle Ed—my father's brother, who I'd later describe as my rich uncle—felt that the most appropriate burial place for Daddy was in my parents' home state, Kentucky. He'd already bought a pricey family plot at Cave Hill, a lush, park-like cemetery in Louisville that's on the National Register of Historic Places. My father would be in good company since Cave Hill would over the years become the final resting place

22

of celebrities including legendary boxer Mohammed Ali, the sisters who wrote the "Happy Birthday to You" song, and Kentucky's most celebrated purveyor of fried poultry.

Ed eagerly paid all the expenses to fly my father's body to Louisville for interment in Kentucky's finest graveyard—and later, when he decided that Daddy's burial spot was getting too much shade, he even paid to move the body to a sunnier location.

My mother didn't care whether her husband was buried in sunshine or shade, or in Kentucky or New York. "It seemed silly to spend all that money to fly John's body down to Kentucky, and then to pay even more to move him to a different plot," she told me years later. "But it was important to Ed, and as long as he was paying for it, it didn't matter to me. He could go ahead and do whatever he wanted to do. It's not like your father would notice the difference."

Her practical approach to life and death was consistent. When I asked her years later how she'd dealt with the simultaneous challenges of losing a husband, finding a job, getting a college degree, and raising a son all by herself, her answer was simple: "You just do what you have to do." Decades later, she admitted that, in some ways, her life actually improved after his death, since she was able to go back to college and create her own career.

Would I be as practical about my mother's decline as she'd been with my father's? Or would I need to find the nearest wall-to-wall blue carpet on which to prance?

3. Nursing Home Hunters

New York City, 2015

Queens Boulevard isn't nicknamed the "Boulevard of Death" because of the nursing home that squats along its heavily trafficked lanes. But that moniker certainly didn't make the idea of moving my mother there any more appealing.

In a way, shopping for a nursing home is like that real-estate show on cable TV, in which cash-laden couples seek the perfect place to call home. The difference is that when it comes to senior living, instead of choosing the property with the prettiest master suite and the best backyard for a swimming pool, you must decide which residence is the least likely to plunge you and your entire family into permanent emotional and economic depression.

So here we were, my sister Glynn and me, the stars of our own imaginary episode of *Nursing Home Hunters*. The goal: find a place in New York City that would take good care of our mother.

A quick survey of facilities near my sister's home in New Jersey revealed that they were no better (or cheaper) than the ones in New York City—and they were further from mass transit, which would make it harder for me to visit since I was a typical, car-free New Yorker. So we set our sights on the sunny streets of Queens, the borough that my husband and

I had called home for the past several years. My sister and I made a string of appointments and then donned comfortable shoes to hit the pavement over the course of two warm June days, clutching a short list of nursing homes that met three main criteria: proximity to where I lived, accessibility to the subway, and generally positive online reviews.

Let the show begin.

Home #1 is an eight-story brick building in a leafy residential neighborhood in Queens. It has a convenient location not far from Mark's home, and lots of amenities that Mark and Glynn both like.

Each of the eight floors at Venerable Hills Care and Rehabilitation Center was self-contained with carpeted hallways, a dining room, library, and multiple lounges furnished with couches and armchairs that you might see in someone's house. Plus, it was pretty close to my apartment. But we needed to see more to make sure this was the right choice.

Home #2 is also conveniently located. But the site inspection gave Glynn and Mark lots to think about ...

A woman who looked like me in drag (complete with poor posture, unflattering miniskirt, and clunky high heels that drew attention to her stringy legs) greeted us in the lobby of LaGuardia Manor Rehab and Nursing Home.

"I don't usually do the tours, so I don't really know much," she offered with an apologetic shrug. "But I can show you around."

We strolled through echo-filled halls and medicine-scented rooms cluttered with giant pieces of wheeled equipment. Then we arrived at a tiny outdoor terrace, which sat on the roof of a low floor behind the main building.

"This is nice," Glynn said, grasping at something positive. "Do you bring residents out here when the weather's warm?"

The woman's eyes widened. "Oh gee, I don't know," she stammered. "I think usually they just put them out on the sidewalk so they can get some sun."

We crossed LaGuardia Manor off our list as soon as we left.

Home #3 is in a desirable upscale Queens neighborhood, and it checks a lot of boxes on Glynn and Mark's wish list. Clean and well-organized, the facility is crowned with a rooftop deck that they both love.

Our guide at Resplendent Care Adult Residence was knowledgeable and thorough. She made no mention of placing residents out on the street. But we were concerned that several rooms had three beds, rather than the customary two.

"How can we make sure our mother would be in a room with only one roommate?" I asked.

"That's determined on a first-come, first-served basis," the woman answered. "We can't guarantee it."

That was a deal-breaker. Resplendent Care was off our list.

Home #4 is a bit farther out in Queens. It's received positive reviews online and has a well-equipped exercise room with lots of natural light and great views.

But Rendezvous Villa Rehabilitation Center was the farthest from where I lived, and the dining room was a windowless affair that resembled a military mess hall on a remote space station, perhaps where an alien might emerge from the abdomen of an unfortunate cafeteria aide.

After making the rounds, Glynn and I sat down in a diner, hamburger grease dripping down our fingers as we reviewed our notes.

"They're all gross and depressing in their own unique way," I said. "But LaGuardia Manor truly makes me want to throw myself into traffic."

"I agree," Glynn said. "The one that's closer to your apartment actually has the best facilities, and it's the closest to where you live."

Home #1, Venerable Hills, indeed, was the most attractive—and most conveniently located—of the bunch that we toured. And with that, we made the decision about where my mother would spend the next phase of her life. Now it was time to let her know.

4. Eunice's Tips for the Perfect Road Trip

(the first in a series of handy, posthumous advice columns, culled from years of listening to my mother)

1. If you're traveling with a kid, keep him entertained. Buy comic books wrapped in plastic and don't let him open them until you get to the interstate—otherwise he'll read them all in the first thirty minutes and then complain about being bored for the next five hours. You don't want to have to deal with that all the way to Ohio, do you?
2. Don't waste money on roadside restaurants. Put a cooler in the back seat and pack plenty of snacks, and maybe a picnic lunch with cold cuts. Potato chips and pop are a must. Don't bother bringing water. Rest stop water fountains are free.
3. You can walk around Stuckey's as much as you want but don't buy the pecan log. I know it looks enticing and we've been seeing billboards about it for the entire trip. But you've never finished one, and I won't either.
4. Turn off the radio and don't talk to me when I'm driving through heavy traffic unless you're helping me navigate.

I don't care if you think Anita Ward's "Ring My Bell" is the perfect musical accompaniment to the curvy highway that wraps around Cincinnati's skyline. I'm trying to drive, and I need to concentrate.

5. The town of Versailles, Kentucky, is pronounced "Ver–SALES," not "Vair-Sigh." And no, I don't care how they pronounce it in France. Don't be a smart aleck. You're distracting me by reading every sign out loud.

6. Don't tell me I can merge onto the thruway right after the AMC Pacer. You *know* I have no idea what an AMC Pacer looks like. Just tell me the color of the car or you'll get us killed!

5. Running from the Ball

Brockport, 1974

The Kendall boy wasn't very tall for a sixth grader, but he was wide. Very wide. And very round. His girth overflowed from beneath his dirty white T-shirt, protruding over his blue shorts like a lava flow encroaching upon a helpless continent. He usually didn't smile, but the slightest of evil grins curled his lips when he learned that the gym teacher had pitted him against me in a wrestling match.

When you're the second-smallest boy in the sixth grade and a decidedly non-athletic one at that, the last thing you want to do is wrestle big, mean boys. I had no idea why the PE instructor decided to place me on the mat with that Kendall boy. Maybe he was trying to toughen me up. Or maybe he was just sadistic. As I got on all fours, my pale, stick-like legs jutting out of oversized piped shorts, I realized that the teacher's motivation really didn't matter. As I waited for the bell, I knew that my goal was simply to stay alive while struggling against a boy whose weight was about three times my own, and whose sullen face clearly indicated he'd love to destroy me in front of the whole class.

The whistle blew, and the kid took his time chipping away at my already challenged masculinity. He wasn't a very good wrestler. But I was much worse, and I looked like a bleached lab rat next to him. Over the course of a few minutes, he repeatedly threw himself on top of me. I flailed, I flopped, I floundered like the scrawniest creature in nature, a pale, red-headed mammal doomed to death beneath a larger predator. Eventually I stopped struggling and accepted defeat, inhaling the odor of the unwashed wrestling mat and the equally unwashed Kendall boy. By that point I didn't even care. I was just happy for it to be over.

My stunning defeat wasn't surprising. I sucked at all sports, and as a result I hated them all—especially anything involving teams since angry teammates could easily blame me for any loss.

My mother, unfortunately, included athletics as a key component of her long-term strategy to expose me to male role models. She wanted me to be happy and well-adjusted and didn't want me to miss out on anything just because I didn't have a father. She wanted me to fit in.

"Since your father's not alive, it's good for you to be around other boys, and some grown-up men too," she explained as she justified my spectacularly unsuccessful forays into a series of extracurricular sporting activities.

The truth is, you can't really miss what you barely ever had. Since I didn't remember much about my father, having just one parent seemed natural to me. I wasn't sitting around craving time with masculine role models. Even though most kids in my school had two parents (divorce wasn't common yet in our small town), the only time my single-parent situation stuck out like a sore thumb was in the male-centric scouting organizations that staged "father/son" activities—which, in my mind, did nothing but draw attention to the fact that I was different from everyone else. I dreaded events like the annual wooden car-racing event, a competition that simultaneously publicized my fatherless state as well as my inability to build anything useful with my hands (although I could draw well. Why didn't they just let us draw?). Since I was always the only kid with no dad in the troop (or den or herd, or whatever they called it), I sometimes had to team up with another scout's father, a well-meaning man who did his best to guide me. "You're going to ruin the wood!" he'd blurt as I half-heartedly sanded a block to create a mangled, sure-to-lose submission for the all-important race.

• • •

My mother's far-reaching masculinization initiative threw me into a never-ending stream of disastrous athletic endeavors. "I know you may not be too interested in football, but just give it a try," she prodded one day while driving me to the initial meeting of a springtime extramural flag football club (or was it intramural? I have no idea. Both terms made me picture kicking a ball alongside the wall of a gigantic, color-fully painted castle, with the vague threat of being sent to the dungeon inside if I didn't perform well).

The Helen Reddy song "You and Me Against the World," which I fantasized was written about my mother and me, played on the radio of Mom's giant, canary-yellow sedan. I wanted to just stare out the window and ponder the touching lyrics about maternal love, and maybe spend the afternoon shopping for beautifully rendered, die-cast toy cars at Long Ridge Mall (yes, I was a bit effeminate, but I loved toy cars, not dolls. Although I also loved playing *I Dream of Jeannie* with my friend Ann). My mother soon interrupted the Aussie pop star's ditty and my daydream about finding a trailer to pair with my toy Studebaker station wagon.

"It's always good to try new things and make some new friends," my mother assured me as she nosed her bulky car into the parking lot. "If it turns out you don't like it, you don't have to sign up again." I could have saved her some time; I knew I wouldn't like it. But I didn't know how to say no.

I didn't like flag football. I *really* didn't like it. My goal on the field was the same as for every team activity: to stay as far as possible from the action at all times. My worst fear was that someone would throw the ball to me, putting me in the frightful position of having to perform some impossible physical feat—unimaginable acts like catching the ball, running with it, and possibly trying to *make a goal or throw it to someone else on our team*. I aimed to stay as invisible as possible.

The words "faggot" and "gay" were thrown about the field, not always directly at me, but at anyone who messed up a shot or a goal or whatever you call the things you're supposed to do on the field. So I heard it a lot. And it's no surprise that some teammates got mad at me because I was following my own strategy of distracted detachment rather than the team's "all-for-one" approach. Still, I stuck through until the end of the semester. And I didn't complain. I was too embarrassed to tell my mother how bad I was.

"Would you like to sign up again for next season?" My mother asked.

"No."

Next, my mother suggested judo classes, where I soon learned that sneaking out to the water fountain was more enjoyable than trying to take down other classmates. The musky smell of the thick judogi outfits and well-used mats reminded me of my stunning loss to the Kendall boy.

And there was the swim team, where I consistently underperformed but at least could enjoy the sight of skimpy swimsuits on the other boys.

I guess I was too ashamed to tell my mother outright that I hated all sports. If she had, at some point, said something along the lines of "maybe you're not built for sports, but that's okay," I might have fessed up. Instead, for several years, it was always a matter of finding some other sporting activity to try. The fact that she never acknowledged my lack of athletic ability made me feel worse. She must have realized how bad I was, and I assumed she was so mortified that even mentioning the topic was forbidden, a horrible family secret that we must pretend didn't exist, like having a crazy relative locked in your attic.

34

• • •

Sports weren't the only tactic my mother tried in her quest to expose me to male role models. A year or two after we moved back into our family home from the apartment complex, she had a big idea: to rent out part of our house to a pair of male college students. By dividing the lower-level family room into a living room and bedroom and installing a shower, stove, and refrigerator in the basement, she could kill two birds with one stone: bring in rental income and also import some masculine grown-ups to soak the house in macho vibes.

The guys were nice enough. But they were clearly busy with studies and socializing and weren't overly interested in being a big brother to a skinny red-headed boy who liked watching sitcoms and drawing airplanes more than playing Frisbee and ogling girls.

The following summer, my mother enrolled me in a summer kids' soccer league that was, surprisingly, almost tolerable, largely because the coach was a college professor who was more sophisticated and less competitive than the ones I'd had on other teams. As a result of his attitude, the other boys were a bit more relaxed too.

Of course, I still sucked and I was still miserable. I don't even have a clue what position they assigned me, but it was one that gave me the least number of opportunities to throw a monkey wrench in the team's overall strategy. I remember my mother sitting on the bleachers during one summer match, the late afternoon sunlight dancing across her close-mouthed smile, which hid the fact that she'd probably rather be reading the novel peeking out of her giant brown purse. Nothing in her jovially round face belied any embarrassment about my reliably subpar performance on the field. She dutifully clapped every time our team scored, even though I never had anything to do with the goal, and—more likely—any victories were actually *in spite of* my deficiencies.

Years later, my mother gave me her candid description of my soccer-filled summer. "I watched all the other boys running around after the ball during those soccer matches," she recalled, laughing. "They never stopped running. Then I'd look at you and you were just kind of standing there, staring into space. I always wondered what you were thinking about."

I was probably daydreaming about my pending early escape from the soccer season. Because no matter how many errors I made on the field, there was a brilliant, shining light at the end of the tunnel: a trip to Kentucky. Best of all, we would have to leave before the league entered its final matches for the season. This early departure was glorious, magnificent, absolute salvation for me since my absence meant the team couldn't blame me if they lost. I watched the calendar like a jailbird counts the days before his release.

Finally, departure day arrived. I turned in my wrinkled soccer uniform and resigned from my position as wingback or center back or whatever. I was now taking on a much more exciting role: that of a passenger, seated next to a fully stocked plastic cooler in the back seat of my mother's hulking sedan. A sweet surge of relief settled upon me as Brockport— with all its menacing soccer balls, frightful footballs, and husky wrestlers—grew smaller in the rear window. Our final destination was a wonderful, warm place where my physical ineptitude was never an issue.

6. Venerable Living

"I ain't never seen a place like *this* before," the young man mumbled as he rolled my mother through the lobby of Venerable Hills, past a bubbling fishpond and a fake fireplace that was almost an exact replica of the one at the assisted living facility that my mother had just moved out of. The other nursing homes I'd toured didn't try as hard as Venerable Hills to create such a comforting environment, and I had to admit it was fairly impressive.

"Is this a hotel?" my mother asked as we crossed the second-floor library to arrive at Room 221, her new home.

"This is actually like the place where you were living upstate," I answered, smiling as I placed what I hoped was a reassuring hand on her shoulder. "But this is better because it's really close to where I live." I tried to speak simply and positively, always avoiding the dreaded term *nursing home*. The brain tumor had affected her thinking, but I was still afraid she might suddenly realize she'd just checked into the last place on Earth that she'd ever want to be. I amped up my smile a bit, just to make sure she knew how absolutely wonderful everything would be.

"Oh, okay. That sounds good," she said, instinctively raising her bony left hand to pat my hand. I stroked her short hair, a salad of brown and gray strands made messy after the long, uncomfortable ride from upstate.

Glowing fluorescent lights lined the wall above the bed in my mother's new room, and a sheer curtain dangled on one side, hiding the bed of the person who would now be her roommate. The other woman wasn't in the room, although an afternoon talk show blared from her TV.

The medical transport aide, who'd ridden with my mother in the van all the way from Rochester, expertly guided my slow-moving mother to her feet and into bed before leaving.

The muted tones of this institutional setting were brightened by the smiling nurse who walked in next. "We've been waiting for you, Mrs. Chesnut!" he said cheerfully as he set a blue plastic tray of food on a rolling table in front of her. "My name is Peter."

"Thank you," my mother smiled, deftly shifting her tone from confusion to a well-tuned autopilot set to Southern politeness. Being agreeable was her standard conversational tactic, whether to show friendly respect or to politely minimize and dismiss conversations that made her uncomfortable. "It's very nice to meet you."

"We thought you might be hungry, so I've brought you a tuna fish sandwich and a few other things," Peter said, placing his hand on her forearm. "I hope that's okay."

"Yes, that sounds very good. Thank you very much."

Peter left, and I was alone with my mother for the first time since her arrival in New York City. Her face still resembled the old photos I'd seen of her as a teenager in Louisville. She still had the expressive, light brown eyes that were vaguely reminiscent of Judy Garland's. Some of her hair was the same mousy brown color as always, with a texture that she always described as "frizzy." She still had the rounded nose and chin, and the quick smile that nowadays was often deployed when she didn't hear or understand what someone said. Her once-plump cheeks had deflated in recent months, while part of her forehead and cheek were swollen and bruised from her recent fall. But her eyes still sparkled when she smiled.

I sat on the bed and took her hand, which was still as soft as when she used to walk me through the Sears and Sibley's department stores in Rochester decades earlier.

"I'm glad to see you, kiddo," she said, patting my hand.

"I'm really glad you're here, Momma." Over the course of my life, I'd progressed from calling her Mommy to Mom to Momma, the last moniker a more recent effort to preserve a bit of our evaporating Kentucky heritage. (My father, meanwhile, was frozen in time as Daddy.)

I unwrapped the sandwich and handed it to her. She took a bite and gave it back to me. "You have some too," she said.

"I'm not really that hungry."

I bit into the moist wheat bread, and the flavor of canned tuna was surprisingly decent.

I passed her a white plastic cup of water. "So how are you feeling? You had a long trip today."

"It was *very* long. I think they gave me something to eat and drink onboard that bus, so at least I didn't starve to death." She took a sip of the water and looked at me. Her brow furrowed. "But you'll have to forgive me that I'm just a little bit crazy. Where am I again?"

"You're at a place called Venerable Hills, in New York City," I answered, stressing the proximity to where my husband and I lived. "Now you're very close to Angel and me, so we can visit you more!"

"But do I *stay* here?"

"Yes. This is kind of like where you used to live in Brockport. But here, they'll pay more attention to you, and you'll be closer to Angel, Glynn, and me. Plus," I smiled, "this place is cheaper, and Medicaid will pay for it."

Venerable Hills actually wasn't cheaper. And it was true that Medicaid would pay for it, but not yet. First, she'd have to exhaust her own savings to almost nothing, a concept called a "spend down." But my mother didn't need to know all that now.

I was following the lesson my mother had taught me ever since childhood: avoid the truth if it will keep someone from feeling bad. Lying is also justifiable if it will get someone to shut up, if they're being annoying or talking about something that makes you uncomfortable. Just yes them to death, she taught me, and eventually the person will shut their trap. I'd been on the receiving end of that strategy with my mother, and it usually worked on me. You can definitely avoid confrontations and discomfort using this tactic, but the downside is that you don't get to address or resolve certain issues in a straightforward way. But today, there was no reason to be overly honest. We were in a horrible, depressing situation, and I wanted my mother to think only happy thoughts.

She smiled and took another bite of the sandwich. "Medicaid will pay for *this*? That's wonderful. I don't want to spend all your inheritance. You might get all of fifty cents if we play our cards right!"

Another nurse entered. "Welcome, Mrs. Chesnut," she said. "How are you? My name is Tina. How was your trip? I understand you've traveled a long way."

"I'm fine, thanks. Just a little tired, but I'm pleased to be here." She was on autopilot again.

"Listen, I hate to interrupt you and your son. I know you have a lot to talk about. We'd just like to do a few quick tests to make sure everything's fine, so we can get you settled into your new place. Would that be all right?"

"Oh *sure*, that sounds like a lot of fun," my mother said, smiling slyly. "It's good to be in demand."

The nurse helped her into the wheelchair and rolled her out.

I was alone in the room. My smile—which had been beaming in a nonstop effort to project a positive vibe powerful enough to heal every illness in the entire nursing home—immediately disappeared. I opened my mother's blue roll-aboard suitcase and unpacked a few things: fuzzy winter hats that she used to wear while brushing the snow off her car during brutal western New York winters. A fuzzy pink bathrobe she preferred to wear when writing or reading in bed. Blouses reserved for semi-formal social events at the historical society where she'd worked as a historian until age eighty-eight. And a sparkly purple sweater that a woman had given her at Chicago's O'Hare Airport after my mother had complimented its beauty while they shared a shuttle cart between gates.

Everything in that suitcase represented a part of my mother's life that had come to an end. Now I had to itemize all the clothes on a yellow form and leave them in a bag at the front desk. The staff would attach labels with her last name so they wouldn't be misplaced on laundry days.

Then I climbed into my mother's bed and slept until she got back from her tests. After she returned, I surrendered the bed, kissed her cheek, and walked back to my apartment. My husband Angel would be home from work soon, and I had a lot to tell him.

I hadn't lived this close to my mother in more than thirty years. And now I was responsible for her life, health, and death, together with my sister, my crucial support teammate in New Jersey. I sat on the couch and fell asleep again until Angel got home.

For the first time, I left my cell phone on all night. I knew I probably wouldn't turn it off again for a very long time.

7. Bluegrass

It was like we lived two different lives: one in the North and
one in the South. And, for all my mother's efforts to expose me
to testosterone in Brockport, I actually already had masculine
role models in Kentucky. All it took was an 800-mile ride for
me to indulge in heaping helpings of familial love and acceptance. Luckily, we made that trip at least two or three times a
year. Of course, having a masculine role model doesn't necessarily mean that dressing in drag is verboten, as I found out
during one lively summer.

In his book *Hillbilly Elegy: A Memoir of a Family and
Culture in Crisis*, author J.D. Vance, who grew up in Ohio
but spent a lot of time in Kentucky with his extended family,
noted that regardless of socioeconomic standing, Kentuck-
ians always make sure—if they move out of state—that they
have the ability to go back home to visit as often as possible.
Our family was no different in that respect (although we were
different in many other ways. If you think you can generalize
about all Southern people, you're wrong).

The Bluegrass State provided me with blissful vacations
for seventeen years. In Brockport, I had to navigate school
settings where I never quite fit in. I was one of the few kids
with no father, the only one with Southern roots, and one of

the few from a Democratic family in a heavily Republican town (which proved especially disastrous when my mother ran for political office). And, of course, I walked funny, sucked at sports, and was one of the few boys who had to wear a T-shirt in the swimming pool since I was a fair-skinned redhead. Some kids on the school bus would purposely slide over in their seats just to make sure I wouldn't sit with them. Boys would call me names and every now and then someone would threaten to beat me up, although thankfully those threats never came to fruition.

It was a different world in Kentucky.

Sure, I didn't fit in much down South, either—there, I was the only Northern kid with a strange accent ("y'all shore do talk funny," my second cousin Jo Frances once told my mother and me). But since my interactions with other children were limited to religious activities at the Holy Heights Missionary Baptist Church, there wasn't time for kids to realize that I sucked at sports, and the presence of my grandparents distracted from the fact that my father wasn't around. Sitting through Sunday school was a cinch compared to throwing a baseball or catching a football. Thanks to my annual attendance at Vacation Bible School, I even memorized—and could sing the names of—all the books of the Bible, no problem at all.

While I did go through a period where I fantasized about moving to Kentucky to be closer to my always-welcoming extended family, as far as I know, my mother never considered moving, even after my father died. She had built a full life in New York State, with lots of friends and activities. Plus, her parents no longer lived in the city of Louisville, where she had grown up, so moving closer to family would have entailed creating a new life in a small town that she'd never called home. So we stayed in the North, and the South provided me with a welcome escape route, several times a year.

• • •

44

After grueling weeks of avoiding that damned soccer ball, my heart soared as we pulled into the circular driveway at my grandparent's house in Benton, the seat of a dry county in western Kentucky where the water was soft, the homes were charming, and the earth was red clay.

The rich scent of knotty wood paneling and sizzling fried chicken greeted my nostrils as we entered the house. Two elderly people, both born in 1898 in rural western Kentucky, were waiting inside. My grandfather—who we all called Pop—was the first to the family room door as we approached, his frazzled gray hair swept messily over his nearly bald head, and his short-sleeved, button-down shirt wrinkled as if he'd just mowed the lawn (which he probably had). His eyes sparkled behind his large gold frames as he gave me a bear hug, and I could feel his sizeable tummy pressing against me.

"We're so glad you're here, pardner," he said. He always called me that.

I ran into the wood-paneled family room where my always-sickly grandmother, who looked worse off than she really was since she was slightly hunchbacked, slowly pushed herself up from the couch, seemingly powered by the bright smile that was growing beneath her broad nose. "Well, hello honey," she said as I gave her a big hug, taking in the aroma of the hair spray that kept her sizeable, salon-styled hairdo perfectly in place. She promised that supper would be ready soon, after which she'd let me choose a game for us all to play; the choices included dominoes, a board game in which we competed to bid on European masterpieces, and a French card game that pitted us against each other in an imaginary road race.

On Sunday, the routine was comfortingly predictable. I put on a jacket and polyester clip-on tie and settled into the prickly, overheated cloth seat of Pop's massive maroon sedan with cool hidden headlights, a car he'd gotten in 1969 and would never replace, and rode to the Holy Heights Missionary Baptist Church, where we greeted every one of his friends before I headed into Sunday school, which was peopled with polite kids who didn't seem to notice that I wasn't paying that much attention to the lesson; I was probably daydreaming about the post-church trip that Pop and I would make to the town dump (up North, garbage trucks picked up our refuse, but Pop dropped his off at the dump, which I found exotic, exciting, and delightfully smelly).

Like any good Southern Baptist, Pop and Gran didn't drink alcohol or go to the movies on Sundays. We weren't allowed to do much of anything on Sundays, in fact, except overeat and visit with uncles and cousins. In other ways, though, Pop wasn't a stereotypical older, straight, Southern man. Like me, he had no interest in playing or watching sports. Instead, we'd plop down with my grandmother on the semi-circular family room couch and watch Lawrence Welk or *Hee Haw* (a show they only watched when I was there).

There were no other kids in my extended Kentucky family, so—just like in Brockport—I used my imagination to stay entertained. I wandered the neighborhood by myself, exploring the musty horse stables in the park behind my grandparents' house and the creek that ran through town. I barreled down the hilly street in front of their home on the super-popular 1970s version of a plastic, low-riding tricycle. I drew cars and airplanes in my sketchbooks. I explored my grandparents' house too; but the most interesting part, in my opinion, was off-limits: my grandparents' bedroom. And that is where I found out that my grandfather was so secure in his masculinity that he'd be willing to dress in drag.

• • •

"Don't go into Pop and Gran's bedroom," my mother warned. "They don't keep their space as clean as the rest of the house. We don't want to be rude and invade their privacy."

Indeed, most of their home was tidy. My grandmother's gold-leafed, Polish-made Walbrzych china set was always on display, ready to host a deluxe dinner at the drop of a hat—accompanied, perhaps, by tinkling music from the cabinet grand piano that sat in the living room. The sparkling pink bathroom smelled of recently sprayed disinfectant and the living and dining areas were kept comfortable with an ever-humming air conditioner. It was a modest home, and every corner was welcoming—except for the room where my grandparents slept.

So that, of course, was where I most wanted to go.

It was a lazy summer afternoon when I decided to venture where no boy had gone before. My mother was reading in the guest room with the door firmly closed. Pop had spent the morning with a wet rag draped over his bald head as he mowed the lawn. Gran would be busy in the kitchen later making fried chicken (yum) and okra (yuck). But for now, they were both snoozing in the family room, Gran slumped over on the semi-circular couch with her lips puffing and Pop in his big leather armchair, snoring so mightily that I could hear it all the way on the other side of the house.

The coast was clear. This was my chance.

Yellow-tinged shadows oozed into the hall when I opened the door to the bedroom, which was gloomily dark even during the daytime since Pop had hung thick drapes over the windows to keep out the scalding summer sun. A swirl of hot air enveloped my arms as I stepped inside, and the scent of moist fabrics and damp wood reached into my nostrils as I gazed up at the ceiling, where ancient water stains had turned an entire corner brown. It was like walking into a completely different ecosystem.

Where to start? I knelt to peer beneath the unmade bed and immediately found a treasure: an old cosmetics case, the kind women who sold makeup door to door used when they visited customers. But there was no rouge in sight; instead, the case overflowed with stale peppermint candy—the soft, unwrapped kind that old people liked. I picked up a piece and gave it a lick. Pretty good. I popped the whole thing in my mouth, enjoying the sensation as the sugary concoction disintegrated on my tongue.

A few inches away I spotted an intriguing circular object painted blue and white.

What is that? A giant gravy bowl?

Oh wait, it's a bedpan.

That was probably for Pop's bathroom emergencies; I didn't know exactly what was wrong with him but he peed a lot, and sometimes he had to rush to the bathroom. Kind of gross to find the bedpan near the candy, but the bowl was empty and looked clean, so I guessed I'd be okay.

I glanced across the room and eyed the closet, which overflowed with a seductive jumble of clothes and fancy boxes that could have provided enough wardrobe options for an entire TV show. Kitty Carlisle and Peggy Cass would have found several episodes' worth of glamour for their appearances on *To Tell the Truth*, my grandparents' favorite game show.

My grandmother hated to throw things out, even though she didn't go out as much as she used to and didn't really need many dress-up clothes. As a result, her wardrobe featured styles from long before I was born. When I was really little, her high heels reminded me of the shoes worn by a famous cartoon duck's girlfriend. But still, all those colors and styles captivated me. You could pick any one of her big, fancy dresses and there'd be a pair of shoes and a hat to match. You just had to look around a lot to find the whole outfit because it was all so messy.

"What are you doing in here, boy?" Pop appeared suddenly and smiled when he saw me sitting on the floor in front of the closet. "You looking for treasure? All you're gonna find in here is a whole lot of *junk*."

Pop was fun. The only thing that got him mad was if I "acted ugly," as he called it—which usually involved me being rude or stealing the handkerchief from his pocket.

"I'm just looking around," I said, throwing one of Gran's most flowery Easter bonnets on my head. "Where'd she get all these hats?"

"Well hee, hee, hee, you look just like Aunt Nancy with that silly thing on your head! Your grandmother hasn't worn those hats in years."

Pop shuffled to the towering dresser, pried off his hearing aid, and picked up a tiny battery.

I jumped up with a hat as grand as a parade float and lifted it to his head. He chuckled. "Well now, do I look beautiful too?"

"You look like you could be my mother!" I grinned. "We should show Mom. I have an idea that will make her laugh."

...

I honestly don't remember exactly what I said to convince my grandfather to don his wife's clothes. I already knew that he was a laidback guy with a lively sense of humor, and he was secure enough to laugh at himself.

Whatever I said worked, anyway, because a few minutes later, my hand rapped on the guest room door. "Just a sec," my mother called from the other side.

The door opened and so did Mom's mouth. Standing before her was a short, stocky seventy-three-year-old man, his thin gray hair peeking out from under a huge, crepe-encased blue hat that resembled a birthday cake. A matching blue dress strained against his potbelly, and his feet bulged from the sides of chunky blue pumps. Linked onto his right arm was my small hand, encased in an oversized white glove that was meant to complement the giant yellow gown in which I swam. Plastic flowers dotted a hat that seemed ready to topple onto my face, and sun-colored high heels offered plenty of room for me to grow. Each of us had a boxy purse dangling from one arm. I extended the glossy cosmetics case toward my mother as my best salesgirl smile spread across my face.

"Good afternoon, ma'am," I chirped. "I'm your neighborhood beauty supply lady, and this is my mother. May we come into your home and show you some of our beauty products? We want to help you be as pretty as you can possibly be."

My mother bent over laughing. "You boys are crazy. You should show Gran!"

When I was in Kentucky, it didn't matter at all if I couldn't catch a football. If I could just make my family laugh, life was good.

• • •

After three weeks in Benton, my mother and I said goodbye and headed north. Traveling between Kentucky and New York State, we often spent a few days in Louisville with two more of my favorite relatives: Uncle Ed and Aunt Agnes. After Daddy died, my uncle and aunt were generous to the point of noticeably improving my standard of living. They sent me money, bought me clothes, took us on vacations, and, years later, paid for half of my college tuition.

Uncle Ed and Aunt Agnes always spoke and moved a mile a minute, talking over each other during phone conversations and in person. While all of my extended family were graced with some form of beautiful Kentucky accent, Agnes's was especially interesting because she pronounced some words in ways that no one else in my family did: she said "sufthin'" instead of "something," "warsh" instead of "wash," and—most brilliantly, in my opinion—"warsheteria" instead of "Laundromat." If someone was a character, she'd say "he's a bird," and if someone wasn't worth a damn, she'd say "he's not worth a tinker's naughty word." With her perennially pink, pinched face, she resembled the actor Gary Sinise if he'd been hanging upside down with all the blood rushing to his head while wearing a tight wig of short, copper-colored curls.

Ed and Agnes were different in other ways too. Unlike my other close relatives, they drank alcohol. They always owned sumptuously appointed, US-made luxury cars—mammoth, four-door sedans with padded vinyl roofs, plush upholstery, and angular taillights that were a modern reimagining of automotive shark fins. You could get lost in the back seat—or the trunk, for that matter. Their cars always made ours seem so, well, dull.

For our road trips to destinations including Florida, Virginia, and Georgia, Ed and Agnes packed their four-wheeled luxury barge with an expensive-looking leather travel bar case filled with big bottles of alcohol, as well as a smaller leather case with prescription medicine from the pharmacy they co-owned. Sometimes when we traveled together, they'd offer my mother some kind of pain-relieving pill, but she always said no. Still, I never saw my uncle and aunt—or anyone else in my family, for that matter—overdo it with alcohol or pharmaceuticals. It just wasn't done.

• • •

"You're getting to be a *big boy* now," Uncle Ed said as he lifted me off the ground in his driveway in Louisville's leafy Highlands neighborhood. "We're going to take you to the mall to get you some *big boy* clothes for school."

Why does he always have to call me a big boy? Does he think I look like the statue of the fat kid at that restaurant he sometimes takes us to?

The next day, we got ready for our big shopping trip to Bashford Manor Mall. Getting there was part of the fun for me since it required a cushy ride in Uncle Ed's sunset gold luxury sedan. Compared to what my mother and grandfather drove, this was like landing in Hollywood and shuttling around with the rich and famous. Plus, they lived in Louisville, a big and exciting city compared to the small towns that my grandparents and my mother and I called home.

Uncle Ed and Aunt Agnes were wealthy; the result (my mother later explained) of having no children and two decent full-time incomes. Their careers—as a newspaper printing manager and a nurse, respectively—began when labor was scarce during World War II. In later years, they invested in a pharmacy. They had money to spend, and they were generous with us, but their ostentatiousness embarrassed my mother.

"Hey Mark, I've got something to show you," Uncle Ed said, grinning as we walked out into the yard. Standing next to his gleaming sedan with his thinning, dyed-black hair and mustache complemented by a multicolored golf cap and over-sized plaid pants with an elastic belt band sewn into the waist, he looked like an aging TV star in search of a golf course cock-tail party (he reminded me of a desperately hipper version of the actor Phil Silvers, if that means anything to you). "Wait here for a minute," he said, motioning for my mother and me to stay in the driveway.

Ed dove into the front seat and soon a bizarre static sound squawked from the front of the car. "HELLO, MARK!" the front grille boomed. "HOW ARE YOU TODAY?" Uncle Ed spoke into a microphone he'd installed on the dashboard, which was connected to a speaker in the grille.

"What on earth ..." my mother murmured, raising one hand to her mouth to cover a smirk.

"Isn't that something?" Ed beamed as he got out of the car. "I had them install a public address system so I can talk to anyone on the street!"

"Well," my mother said, one hand still over her mouth. "You've really outdone yourself, Ed."

"That's really cool!" I gushed. "Can I try it?"

After I announced my name to the entire neighborhood from the car's dashboard, we all piled in, my mother and I sinking into the supremely cushioned back seat; I was still so short that Ed and Agnes were barely visible over the impossibly tall front bench seat. My mother seemed to slump a little, as if she were afraid that someone might see her if Uncle Ed decided to use the public address system while driving. But I was in heaven. Ensconced in this dreamy luxury car, I was about to be spoiled yet again. I could already hear the jingle of the change in Uncle Ed's large pockets, which signaled that he was itching to buy me new clothes for school, and quite possibly a toy or two.

Back at home, after reviewing bags of new clothes from Bacon's and from Stewart's (I loved how back then every city had its own unique department stores), Ed and Agnes sat in the living room and turned on a football game. Boring. But they never seemed to mind that I didn't pay attention when they watched sports. I took a stroll around their two-bedroom, vaguely Tudor home. Their urban lifestyle fascinated me. They were my only close relatives who lived in a city, and the only ones with a home security alarm system and tandem garage in the basement, where one car parked behind the other, rather than side by side. Even their décor seemed cosmopolitan and sophisticated. They'd hired an interior decorator, which my mother said was proof that they had no taste of their own, but I considered it a sign of urban sophistication. Only people on TV and in movies had interior decorators, after all, and only my uncle and aunt had a living room where the pattern on the armchairs matched the couch, and where the glass flower display mimicked the design of the art prints on the wall.

"Free spank!" Aunt Agnes called out as I walked past her, swatting my small fanny as she unwittingly mimicked a James Brown-style grunt. This was one of her favorite ways to interact with me.

I walked to the giant telephone, which was an exotic dark green that I'd never seen anywhere else. I picked up the receiver and held it to my face as if I were a very important big-city dweller about to call some very important big-city friend. Instead, I made a face, hung up, and tip-toed over to my mother, who sat in a corner reading, ignoring the football game that so enraptured my uncle and aunt.

"Hey Mom," I whispered, leaning over into her lap like bored boys do. "Why does their phone receiver always smell like throw-up? It smelled the last time we were here too."

"Shhh!" she hissed, gently swatting me away. "They're going to hear you!"

The following day, we all performed the ritual required of the four of us on every visit to Louisville: a trip to my father's grave at the lushly landscaped Cave Hill Cemetery. Built in the nineteenth century, the Victorian-era facility is something of a tourist attraction thanks to its picturesque landscaping and museum-worthy monuments to the state's rich and famous. We cruised by the Corinthian columns at the main entrance and passed perfectly manicured bushes, several rows of massive tombs and gaggles of geese congregating around a peaceful pond before we reached the newer area, where the monuments and trees were smaller. Ed stopped the car in front of the stone that read Grider Chesnut, named for Agnes's family and ours.

We stood there in the warm August sunlight, making small talk as we stared at the rather plain slab. Agnes bent over to pull a couple of weeds. There was a blank space of earth next to Daddy for my mother, but Mom had already told my sister and me that she wasn't interested in being buried there, or anywhere else, for that matter. She preferred cremation— but we weren't supposed to talk about that in front of Uncle Ed and Aunt Agnes since they'd paid for the plot ("maybe we can just sublet my space to other dead people," my mother would joke when we were alone).

I liked going to see the grave, but I got bored quickly. There's only so much you can do or say when you're visiting a dead body, and I didn't really have any memories to share about him. There were other monuments nearby that were far more interesting.

"Can we go see the other grave now?" I asked. My mother knew exactly what I was talking about. The renowned fried chicken guru hadn't passed away yet, but he'd already built a stately site, complete with soaring columns and a marble bust of his head.

"Sure, kiddo," my mother answered, patting my shoulder. "His grave is a lot more impressive than this one, isn't it?" She cast a glance at my uncle and aunt, who were several steps away, picking at the weeds. "I just hope Uncle Ed doesn't make any announcements over the loudspeaker before we leave the cemetery. He could wake the dead with that thing."

8. Bumps in the Road

New York City, July 2015

If you fly over Jackson Heights on approach to LaGuardia Airport, the Queens neighborhood appears as a cluster of leafy blocks pierced by dozens of brick apartment buildings. Developed in the early twentieth century, the neighborhood still maintains much of the greenery and landmarked architecture that first allowed it to be dubbed the nation's first "garden apartment" community.

And if you had happened to be flying overhead on one particular summer afternoon in 2015 and happened to be carrying binoculars or were graced with exceptional eyesight, you might have witnessed what appeared to be me dumping my wheelchair-bound mother into oncoming traffic.

I wasn't really trying to kill my eighty-nine-year-old Momma, of course. It was the first day that I'd taken her out of the nursing home, and I was still learning how perilous New York City sidewalks could be for wheelchairs. That's the kind of thing you don't really realize until you're pushing someone down the street.

I'd started out with the best intentions. With that nasty brain tumor taking an increasing toll on my mother's memory, I thought that seeing the neighborhood might help her to better grasp the recent changes in her living situation.

Seeing first-hand how close my husband Angel and I lived might provide some comfort too.

You've got to follow the rules if you want to take someone out of a nursing home, even if it's just for an hour or two. I filled out a form at the second-floor nurse's station and then another at the lobby reception desk, accepting full responsibility for my mother's wellbeing while we were gone. Then the sliding glass doors parted and suddenly we were free. The sun and the warm breeze caressed my mother's face for the first time since her arrival in the Big Apple a couple of days earlier. She smiled.

"Isn't it a beautiful day, Momma?" I said, patting her bony shoulder as I gazed at the green leaves swaying above us.

She wrapped her slender hand around mine. "Yes, it is. We're having a *big time*," she said, the last two words mimicking the Kentucky accent and terminology of her youth.

I felt a rush of optimism as we moved past the manicured shrubs and vibrant flowerbeds of nearby residences. *We'll make the best of the situation*, I assured myself. Taking her out today was proof that I could integrate my mother into my life. Angel and I could invite her to dinners at our apartment. I could take her on errands and maybe even to visit nearby friends. Why not? *Life won't be so bad for her here.*

The wheelchair glided over cracks and bizarrely angled pieces of concrete that acted like speed bumps in the wide gray sidewalk. I was flying high on my positive thoughts—and silently congratulating myself on being such a wonderful son—as we descended a ramped area to cross the street.

Then, *WHAM.*

The front wheels ran straight into a sizeable bump where the sidewalk met the pavement. The chair slammed forward. My mother grabbed both armrests and pushed her feet against the pedals, using what must have been a tremendous amount of strength to stay in place as I labored to return the wheelchair to a more upright position. Thanks to her efforts—not mine—she stayed in the seat and avoided landing on the pavement.

I didn't realize there'd be bumps in the road.

"Oh my gosh, Momma, I'm so sorry," I said, pulling her back against the chair. "Are you okay?"

"I'm fine." She laughed, her eyes sparkling behind tinted glasses. "This just adds to the excitement of being outdoors."

"I hope you're not going to tell the people where you live that your abusive son is trying to murder you by pushing you into traffic."

"Oh, and you'll get so much money if you *do* kill me!" I could see the smile curling around her face as we continued our ride across the street and into a pizzeria. She hadn't had much of an appetite since arriving in New York City, but she humored me by eating one greasy, envelope-thin slice of pizza, accompanied by half a bottle of cola, her all-time favorite beverage.

After lunch, we resumed our precarious journey along the pockmarked sidewalks, the aroma of South Asian produce tickling our noses as we passed one of several shops that served the neighborhood's decidedly international community.

"It's very pretty around here," my mother said, her hands tightly grasping the armrests (she probably worried that I might try to dump her again). "Tell me again what this place is called?"

"We're in a neighborhood called Jackson Heights, in Queens, in New York City. Angel and I live here, just a few blocks away."

I didn't bother going into detail about the neighborhood's history, and how a company called the Queensboro Corporation had developed this entire district in the early twentieth century with a bunch of six-story complexes that they dubbed "garden apartments" designed to attract middle-class and upper-middle-class New Yorkers. My husband Angel and I bought a co-op apartment there in 2002, when we realized that our money went further in the thirty-six-block land-marked historic district than anywhere in Manhattan (and most of Brooklyn). In the early twenty-first century, Jackson Heights had become one of the world's most internationally diverse neighborhoods, as well as the gayest area in New York City outside of Manhattan.

Jackson Heights was a perfect neighborhood for me because of my job. As a full-time travel writer, it only made sense to live close to an airport, and we were just ten minutes by bus from LaGuardia. But my travels were on hold for now; I'd decided to abstain from traveling for three months so that I could help my mother get settled into her new living situation. For now, my traveling consisted of simply wandering the shady streets and admiring the lovely architecture of Jackson Heights. I just needed to get the hang of doing it while pushing a wheelchair with a fragile passenger.

I leaned forward to push as the sidewalk angled steeper. Just as we reached the top of the block, my right leg vibrated. My cell phone. We stopped under the shade of a giant tree, not far from the gaze of a pair of stone griffins that adorned the entrance to a nearby apartment building. I pulled out the phone.

"Mr. Chesnut? This is the insurance company calling you back regarding Eunice Chesnut's account," the voice said.

This was one of several calls I'd gotten regarding my mother's affairs. It takes a lot of paperwork to get old and infirm. There are legal and financial issues that need attention—change of address notifications, bank account closings, insurance policy cancellations, that sort of thing. My sister and I handled as much as we could for her, but my mother's memory was slipping and that made it more difficult.

I should have known there'd be bumps in the road.

In some ways, my mother had planned well for this day. A couple of years earlier, she placed my sister's and my name on her bank accounts. That made it easier for me to pay her monthly nursing home bill. We were a team, overseeing a shrinking estate that was never that big in the first place. She'd paid about $3,000 a month out of her own pocket to live at the assisted living facility upstate, and now was forking over some $10,000 every month at the nursing home. The "spend down" would now force my mother to exhaust nearly all her savings in order for Medicaid to kick in and pay the nursing home bills. Given her meager funds, it wouldn't take long to reach that point.

We had to make a lot of changes. Whether it was a bank or an insurance company, the telephone routine was always the same. I'd need to put my mother on the line so that she could confirm personal details and authorize the representative to speak with me.

She had a brain tumor, not Alzheimer's or dementia (at least as far as we knew—over the past year or so, she'd started refusing extra tests because she said it wasn't worth diagnosing something she didn't want treatment for). But the effects were similar. I raced against the clock of my mother's dwindling alertness to wrap up her affairs. At what point would she no longer be able to recite her name, social security number, birthdate? What would happen if she couldn't confirm her own identity? Should I just pretend to *be* her on the phone, imitating her nasal Midwestern accent paired with a few Southern inflections? When I was a teenager I used to mimic her speech patterns just to make fun of her (I was a rotten kid sometimes). And I got pretty good with my impression. How would some random insurance agent know that I wasn't her?

I decided to be honest and handed the phone over to her.

"Momma, it's your insurance company calling," I explained. "Remember how we need to change your address since you moved? They just want you to answer some questions and say that it's okay for them to speak with me about your account."

"What do I need to tell them?" She hesitated before taking the phone. "You know I can't remember anything anymore."

"Don't worry," I said, masking my concern. "It's just the basic stuff like your name, birthdate, and social security number."

Her skinny hand twisted awkwardly around the iPhone, as if she were trying to reach around the corner of a building. "Hello?" She turned to me. "I can't hear anything, sweetie."

I moved the phone to the palm of her hand and then closer to her ear.

Suddenly the humid summer air felt stickier.

My mother frowned as she listened to the voice. "Yes, this is she," she said, followed by her birthdate and social security number. "Yes, that's fine, my son may speak with you about all of that. I give you my permission. Thank you, you too."

I breathed a sigh of relief as I took the phone and finished the call. My mother sat quietly, watching passersby. After ten minutes, we were done. "I'm sorry that took so long, Momma. Since it's so hard to get people on the phone, I didn't want to miss that call."

"It's okay, sweetie. Now who was it again that you were talking to?"

"It was the insurance company. They just needed some more information to change your address."

"Oh, well, that's good. I appreciate you taking care of that."

"I couldn't do it without you, Miss Eunice. So ... now that we're done with all that boring stuff, would you be interested in rolling over to see where Angel and I live? It's just a couple blocks from here."

She looked in the direction that I pointed in and pursed her lips. "Actually, sweetie, I think I'd rather go back home now. I'm kind of tired."

• • •

Nursing homes are decidedly different from assisted living facilities, and they're designed for different types of residents.

August Village, the assisted living facility where my mother had lived upstate, looked a lot like an apartment building. A grand piano sat in the richly carpeted lobby, complemented by comfy couches, a brimming bookshelf, and an inoperable-but-attractive fireplace. Multiple chandeliers illuminated the spacious, carpeted dining room, which looked out on a fenced-in pond where ducks paddled contently. The small activity room offered a variety of art supplies and party supplies; they even had wigs that would have been perfect for impromptu drag shows.

On the second floor, residents and visitors alike could relax in the carpeted TV lounge or head into the library to read or play board games. Books were arranged by category, including a large section filled with titles that my mother thought were trashy.

"Yuck!" she said after scanning the garish collection of bodice-ripper romance novels. "You'll never catch me reading any of those!"

My mother's room at August Village was a pleasant, carpeted studio, complete with a kitchenette equipped with a sink, microwave, and refrigerator. The only way you might guess that this wasn't a "regular" apartment was that it had no stove, and there were safety bars in the bathroom and emergency pull cords next to the toilet and bed.

Now, it was time for Angel, Glynn, and me to transform her new room in New York City into something like home. We hung up a print of the Morgan-Manning House, the gorgeous, Victorian-era mansion where my mother had served as historian for more than thirty years. We plopped framed family photos on her nightstand and dresser. We connected the television and phone. We set up folding chairs so the whole family could sit around her bed at the same time.

But the framed print kept sliding off the wall. The photos on the table kept toppling over. My mother couldn't hear the phone ringing and didn't remember how to answer it, or even speak into it if we handed her the receiver. And a nurse informed us that extra furniture wasn't allowed, because it might block access to the bed. I took the chairs back to my storage unit and disconnected the phone.

• • •

The lack of homey décor didn't really matter, I guess. My mother didn't seem to notice anything missing, and when we returned from our bumpy outing we simply stared at some muted TV talk show while we chatted. After a few minutes, a well-dressed woman with sand-colored hair and glasses entered and introduced herself as Susan. She turned to my mother.

"If it wouldn't be too much trouble, would you mind if I steal your son for a little while, Mrs. Chesnut? Then we'll both come back and see you too."

"Fine, fine." My mother smiled.

I followed Susan to her small office on the first floor. I soon learned that our impromptu meeting was about a topic that I thought we'd already taken care of. Years earlier, my mother had filled out a pile of end-of-life paperwork, forms with ominous titles like *Do Not Resuscitate*, *Living Will* and *Power of Attorney*. Her main directive to us had been clear for decades: no life support. Pull the plug. She'd already visited enough elderly friends in hospitals and nursing homes to know that she didn't want to pointlessly extend her life.

"I understand that your mother has already completed the forms," Susan acknowledged with a polite smile. "But we need to have new ones signed to indicate exactly what this facility can and can't do for her, in the event of any specific circumstances that might occur." She handed me a sheet with a surprisingly long list of "what ifs" (pleasantries like "patient is unable to eat," "patient is unable to breathe"), each of which required a separate answer. I had to choose whether or not my mother wanted a "natural death."

"That means the staff would let nature take its course," Susan explained. They wouldn't step in with life-sustaining drugs or treatment. I liked the term natural death. It was exactly what my mother wanted, especially now, so I quickly checked that box.

It was dinner time by the time we completed all the paper-work, so Susan accompanied me to the second-floor dining room. Dishes clanged from the kitchen and my mother sat alone, picking at the remains of a nearly empty food tray.

"Hello, Mrs. Chesnut," Susan called out as she moved the tray to a nearby table and set the pile of forms in front of my mother. She launched into what was almost a word-by-word repeat performance of what she'd just told me. But I must give Susan credit. This time, she said everything slower and louder, carefully pronouncing every word, which was the best way to assure that my mother could hear and understand.

"Does all of this sound okay, Mrs. Chesnut? Do you have any questions?"

"If Mark says it's okay then it's okay," she said, pen in hand. "Now where do I sign?"

"Right there, where my finger is," Susan pointed.

Slowly and deliberately, my mother moved her bandaged hand near the paper. But the fingers holding the pen were nowhere near the signature line. She moved it again. Still way off. It was like one of those arcade games, where you can never quite maneuver the robot arm to the right place in order to grab the prize.

I pointed too, as if my finger would somehow be more effective than Susan's. "Right there, Momma, can you see the line?"

"I'm trying."

Another move, even further from the line. I couldn't tell if her inability to sign was because of cataracts, the bandaged hand, or general confusion.

Of course there are bumps in the road.

"That's okay, Mrs. Chesnut," the social worker interrupted. "You can just sign anywhere on the page."

Finally, the pen reached the paper, and a vague autograph appeared. It was not the signature of the woman who'd raised me. But it was okay. Sometimes you just have to deal with the bumps and keep moving forward.

9. The Texas Sheet Cake Massacre

Brockport, 1975

"Whatever you do, don't put your foot in the cake," my mother warned as she laid the still-warm Texas sheet cake inside her giant sedan.

I'm not sure why she'd placed her latest culinary creation on the floor of the front seat, and I'm not sure why I thought it was a good idea to sit with my legs splayed around the cake like an eleven-year-old, bow-legged jockey. It would have made sense for one of us—either me or the dessert—to take the back seat. But like competitive siblings on a road trip, we both just *had* to be in front.

Making food for friends was one of my mother's things. If she cooked a big dinner for the two of us, she'd sometimes make extra to share later. Or she'd whip up a complete dessert for a friend for no particular reason. Sometimes she'd make the ugliest possible fudge you could imagine; a concoction that resembled hard, brown molten lava or perhaps hardened goo from a 1950s science fiction movie, frozen in place on a dinner plate (I don't know why she always poured it onto a dinner plate) with a primordially uneven surface that could have easily hidden ancient fossils from the La Brea tar pits. But what the fudge lacked in presentation, it more than made up for in sugary goodness.

On this warm summer day, the recipient of her gastronomical benevolence was Estelle, one of her best friends, who lived with her college professor husband in a big farmhouse about a mile from our house. Estelle was smart and funny, but my mother said that eating wasn't always a priority for her, so she was the most frequent beneficiary of my mother's culinary generosity.

Today, the featured dish was Texas sheet cake, a thin chocolate confection supposedly invented in the Lone Star State as a variation on German sweet chocolate cake. I didn't particularly care for it (I prefer a regular brownie, which is denser, or a standard cake, which is lighter), but my mother's friends seemed to love the recipe. Texas sheet cakes are also easily transportable, thanks to their single-layer format, so they were easy to deliver.

I didn't care for the cake, but I liked Estelle and her husband Reginald a lot. They were generous people. I especially loved it when they treated us to dinner at the Bradford House, a restaurant located inside the local Grants discount department store. It was even more exciting when I was little because the kiddie menu was printed on a plastic hand puppet that for some reason depicted a pilgrim child named Bucky Bradford. I had no idea who that well-buckled kid was, but I never turned down a free toy—or free food (that's a policy I still follow today as a travel writer).

Estelle always talked to me as if I were a grown-up. She'd ask my opinion about movies, TV, even politics. And I liked all of those cats, even though some of them hissed if you tried to get close. So my mother's invitation to ride with her to deliver the cake was enough to make me stop drawing airline logos in my bedroom, throw down my pencil, and run downstairs. I didn't even bother to put on my sneaks. It was late summer, so my feet had already attained their seasonal numbness to the hard gravel driveway, and I bounded over to the shiny yellow vehicle.

I plopped onto the blue vinyl seat, jutting one bare foot onto the middle of the humped floor and the other against the door.

"Now be careful!" my mother said as she revved the engine. "Estelle's waiting for us. If you're going to sit in the front, *do NOT put your foot in the cake!*"

"Okay, okay, I won't! Jeez, Mom." I spread my legs farther apart, lowering my body in the seat like a spider as I slowly pulled the door closed. I turned the dial on the radio and pushed the black plastic buttons until I found "The Hustle" by Van McCoy. I loved that song because they played it all the time on the radio when we were driving down to Kentucky that summer.

The car inched into the turnaround. Since we lived on a country highway with an unbelievable seventy-mile-per-hour speed limit, the only way to get out safely was to charge forward as quickly as possible. If you tried to pull out slowly or back out tail first, you might get rammed by a giant truck barreling down the road.

Mom stepped on the gas and the car surged into the road in a tight left turn. Suddenly, everything moved in slow motion. My gangly, flailing legs took on a life of their own. They flew up. They circled around. They flew down. And ... SPLAT. They landed squarely in the Texas sheet cake. All the well-planned goodwill and friendship that my mother had baked into that scrumptious dessert collided with the uncontrollable reality of having an eleven-year-old son.

Time returned to normal as I looked up. My mother's face was red as she pulled the car onto the shoulder.

"GOD DAMMIT TO HELL. I TOLD YOU NOT TO PUT YOUR FOOT IN THE CAKE!"

"I'm ... sorry ... Mom." Tears welled up as I stared at my frosting-encrusted toes.

We went home, damaged cake in tow.

• • •

69

Even with all that yelling and swearing, I didn't really have to worry much about the consequences of my culinary destruction. No matter the crime, there was never any formal punishment in our house. She'd swear. I'd cry. And that was about it.

Such was life in a single-parent household with only one kid at home (at least that's how it was for me). You don't need set punishments or rules, for that matter, because there's no extra kid around to complain if someone is treated differently.

I had no regularly assigned chores (except when she told me to mow the lawn), no curfews, no fixed bedtime, no formal punishments (other than getting yelled at), and no allowance. My mother made sure that I was aware of our economic limitations—she was a single woman working part-time, and we made ends meet partially with social security benefits and the veteran's pension from my dead father. I'd ask for money when I wanted it, and as long as the request wasn't extravagant, Mom would usually fork over the cash.

In addition to lax regulations, brand-name food was another perk of living in a two-person household. My mother loved to eat, and for decades she never quite lost the pounds she'd gained from being pregnant with me. She was frugal, to be sure, but the economics of having only two people in the house made it unnecessary to buy bulk quantities of budget-priced products.

She didn't buy powdered drink mixes or generic soda pop; we tickled our noses with the sumptuous froth of brand-name cola. She didn't buy cheap store-brand snacks; we feasted on sandwich cookies from elegant small white packages and glistening boxes with names you'd actually see in TV commercials. My mother refused to buy large boxes of cereal. ("I won't eat any of it, and you wouldn't be able to finish a whole box by yourself before it goes stale.") Instead, she bought me variety packs of tiny boxes with perforated lines so you could open them and eat right from the box. Other kids had to wait until they finished one brand before trying a different cereal, but I could have breakfast with a different brand every day. It was glorious.

My friends were jealous (although to be honest, I sometimes lusted after the food that "normal" kids had in their homes). Whenever a friend stayed overnight, my mother left soft and warm donuts from Wegmans, the trend-setting supermarket chain that everyone from the Rochester area loves, on the dining room table in the morning. My eighth-grade best friend, also named Mark, drooled over my mother's home-made creations—things like gooey grilled cheese sandwiches with ham and even that notoriously ugly fudge.

He also adored my mother's rich Texas sheet cake. It tasted better, of course, when my foot wasn't in it.

10. Quiz Show

New York City, August 2015

Countless wrinkles graced the sea of faces in the TV lounge. Some creases framed warm smiles. Some accentuated tired eyes, while other eyes sparkled. The wrinkles ran down necks, disappearing beneath blouses and shirts before emerging on hands that rested on the arms of wheelchairs. There must have been countless stories behind the well-worn faces in the lounge at Venerable Hills that day. But for now, almost every one of them was turned to the oversized face of the woman who dished out the latest celebrity gossip on the large-screen TV that hung on the wall.

My visits to the nursing home had started to follow a routine. I always stopped at a neighborhood convenience store first to buy a small bottle of cola (my mother's main vice) as well as what had only recently become her favorite snack: sour-cream-and-onion-flavored potato chips. Strolling toward my mother's new residence, I'd instinctively begin practicing the smile that I'd plaster to my face as soon as I entered.

Decades earlier, my mother had trained me to look chipper in gloomy situations. "These people don't have much to look forward to," she had told me when we walked through an echoey nursing home about twenty-five years earlier, on our way to visit an elderly member of our church. "I always smile and say hello to everyone, even if I don't know who they are. It might be the only time anyone speaks to them all day. It would be so depressing to just sit there like that, all alone."

Yet now it was my mother who sat in a nursing home all alone, even as she was surrounded by other residents in the cacophonous TV room.

. . .

If you want to feel powerless, try walking into a nursing home lounge and looking into the faces of its residents. Try imagining who they are—who they *really* are and what their lives were like in the years before they landed in that wheelchair. In this lounge sat women and men of various colors, ethnicities, and nationalities. Some were younger than you might expect to see in a nursing home. Some looked attentively at the television, while others seemed half asleep. But they all had stories. They all had fading histories.

I knew there was nothing I could do to ease the physical and mental decline of these residents. But maybe I could make them feel better, however briefly, if I did what my mother had taught me, long before she became a resident herself: smile and be friendly.

Inspired by the politicians of the day, I donned the persona of Hillary Clinton as I worked my way through that blaring TV lounge, exuding all the positive, people-pleasing energy she brought to campaign rallies. My eyes widened with delight as I jovially pointed toward anyone who made eye contact with me. I reached out to shake hands, pat shoulders, and call a few people by name.

"How's your eye, Mr. Santiago?" I asked one gentleman. "That's a lovely sweater, Patricia!" Patricia was an elderly Long Island native; I sometimes offered to push her in her wheelchair to the dining room for meals (she could never remember my name, and once called out "Son! Son! Son!" to get my attention when she saw that I'd brought chips and dip). I gave a firm pat on the shoulder to Diego, a former hypnotist who was my mother's next-door neighbor and one of the few middle-aged male residents on the floor. And I always made sure to touch the hand of a wheelchair-bound woman named Sue Ann, carefully asking her questions that I knew would elicit a positive answer, since the only response she seemed able to provide was a thickly Queens-accented "yeah," accompanied by a bright grin.

An aide sitting in the back of the lounge looked up briefly when she heard the conversations, then returned to tapping on her cell phone.

My rendition of the woman who might have been president ended when I got to the far side of the room, where my mother sat, shrunken in her wheelchair, staring out the floor-to-ceiling window, oblivious to what played on TV. I knew she wouldn't notice me until I was standing right in front of her. I kneeled right in front of her, a couple of feet away, so I wouldn't startle her.

"Oh thank god," she exclaimed when she finally looked my way. Those three words, recited quickly as if they were just one, had become her standard greeting whenever I arrived. I wrapped my fingers around her veiny hand as she extended it toward me.

"How are you, Momma?" I gave her a kiss on the cheek and a hug, feeling her ribcage against my chest.

"I'm so confused," she said, putting a bandaged hand up to her slender cheek. "I don't know where I am, and I'm afraid they won't know where to come get me."

"Why don't we roll on over to someplace where we can talk, and we'll figure everything out."

"That's a wonderful idea," she said, looking around the room as if she'd just realized where she was. "Let's get out of here."

In addition to my mother's room, we had a choice of two areas designed for socializing. Visitors and residents filled the library that day, so we headed to the sunroom (I don't really know if that's what the room was called, but sunlight shone through a row of large windows onto a collection of plants, so I think that's the vibe they were going for). I said hello to the middle-aged woman who always wandered the floor, using one foot to propel her wheelchair. She was carefully watering the plants with a large plastic watering can; I wondered how she got that job since the other residents didn't have any assigned tasks. The woman never spoke so I couldn't ask her, but she always nodded her head to greet me, and I appreciated that she often moved chairs out of the way to make room for my mother's wheelchair on the days that they shared a table in the dining room.

The celebrity disher's voice was still audible from the TV down the hall and there was occasional clanging of medical supplies from the nurse's station, but it was relatively quiet in the sunroom. I took a seat on the overstuffed couch and handed her the cola and potato chips. She smiled. "Why thank you, sweetie."

She was upset because she was confused, so I knew I needed to slide into what I called game-show mode.

"So what are you confused about, Miss Eunice?" I said with a mock Southern accent. Reverting to our family's Kentucky speech patterns was a common tactic for lightening the mood.

"Well ... I'm just crazy," she said, reaching into the green bag of chips. "I'm not sure where I am, or where I'm supposed to be, or if anyone knows how to find me."

"I bet you know more than you think you do," I said, smoothing her short, curly hair that resembled a frayed tapestry made from grey and coffee-colored threads. "Let's see what you remember. Is it okay if we do the Quiz Show now to see what you know?"

"I guess so. But I'm telling you I don't know *nuthin'*," she replied, pronouncing the last word like her long-deceased father would have.

I'd invented the Quiz Show as a calming exercise to alleviate my mother's nervousness. If she'd been oblivious to the memory loss and confusion that her brain tumor caused, her current situation wouldn't have been as difficult. But she knew she was losing her mental abilities, and that tormented her.

I launched into a series of easy questions to prove that her mind was still working.

"Okay Momma. Let's start with this first. You're staying in a place called Venerable ...?"

"Hills!" she called out, her eyes widening as if she'd been the first contestant to hit the buzzer.

"That's right!" I felt like I should be handing over a crisp $50 bill or lighting up a big board on the wall. Instead, I just grabbed a potato chip and rewarded myself with its salty goodness.

"But is this where she lives?" My mother had started having difficulty with pronouns. But I knew what she meant.

"Yes, it is. And you're very close to where *I* live, so I can come see you all the time. I visit you every day or two. And remember Angel, my husband? He visits you every weekend, and Glynn comes every other weekend, since she lives farther away, in New Jersey."

"Well, that's good." She sat back and looked around the brightly lit room, smiling at a nurse's aide who pushed a wheeled electronic contraption down the hall.

"But where am I supposed to *be*?" She turned back to me. "Do people know where I am so they can come and get me for supper?"

"Of course, Momma. There's always someone who knows where you are, and I always know where you are too. You know I never have trouble finding you when I visit, right? You're always right where you should be."

"Well, I'm glad because I honestly don't know where I am sometimes."

My game show plan had gotten sidetracked a bit. But she needed to have her fears assuaged. And I still knew that if I could get her to travel further back in time, the vibrant details of her youth would come to life and provide a comforting distraction, if only momentarily.

77

"Let's do some more Quiz Show! Can you tell me where you were born?"

She raised an index finger as if pointing at her answer in the air. "Louisville, Kentucky."

"What was the street address where you grew up?"

She nodded her head to confirm she knew this one too. "1004 South 40th Street."

She brightened up when I asked about the nicest department stores in Louisville in the 1940s.

"There were beautiful stores up and down 4th Street," she said. "We didn't go very often, but we'd make a day of it, take the streetcar in the morning and have lunch downtown. We had to wear high heels and gloves just to go shopping." She glanced at the slip-on shoes that a nurse's aide must have placed on her feet that morning. "I'd get home and my feet would be killing me. It made no sense to have to wear something so uncomfortable to do something you like."

"What about after you got married? Where did you live first with Daddy?"

"I don't remember." She took a swig of cola.

"It was Atlanta, wasn't it? You moved there so Daddy could study?"

"Oh yes. I hated living there. Not because I didn't like Atlanta, but because I had no social life. We moved there so your father could get his master's degree in English at Emory University. I worked as a secretary at the college and the people weren't very friendly."

She liked their next home better. After my father took advantage of the GI Bill to get his master's degree, they moved north so that he could start on a PhD at the University of Michigan in Ann Arbor. They moved into West Court, a residential development at Willow Run, an airport and munitions manufacturing complex built in the early days of World War II.

"We really enjoyed living there," she said. "We made lots of friends, and I also made friends at the university. I was a secretary there. It was a happy time."

She was apprehensive about the next move, to Brockport, a quaint college town with lovely Victorian architecture set along the banks of the Erie Canal. There, John would begin his career as an English literature professor. "At first, I didn't know if I'd like living in a small town, but within a few months, I loved it," my mother said, her hand angled strangely as she used her pinkie to wipe potato chip crumbs off her ribbed sweater. "The people were friendly, and we liked the small-town atmosphere."

As she had in Atlanta and Ann Arbor, my mother worked as a secretary in Brockport—first for a college dean and later at the college library. "We really enjoyed our social life with the townspeople and with college faculty members," she said.

It was there in Brockport that John and Eunice Chesnut started building a family when my sister Glynn was born in 1951. They gave up on having more kids when the doctor said that my mother wouldn't be able to. But hey, I just couldn't resist the opportunity to be the center of attention. My mother had one of those unexpected, later-in-life pregnancies, nearly thirteen years later, when she was thirty-nine and my father was in his late forties. "I wouldn't say you were a mistake," my mother had said when, as a teenager, I finally figured out that I was unplanned. "You were a very pleasant surprise."

I wanted to cover some of that territory now, in the sunroom, but it would have to wait. My mother slowly folded the bag of chips shut and took a deep breath. "You've made me feel better with your good conversation," she said, pointing down the hall with a crooked finger, "Now, I really have to go to the toilet."

11. The Embarrassing Footwear Collection

Brockport, New York, 1976

A dramatic, unfamiliar voice slithered through the air as my mother pushed open the screen door with her elbow and gingerly stepped into the living room, balancing a pair of grocery bags that threatened to tumble from her arms.

"Hellooooo Derwood!" the voice intoned, dripping with attitude.

At first, my mother couldn't see who was talking. Her eyes scanned the living room and made their way up the wall to the ceiling, where she finally found the source of the bizarre salutation: it was me, ensconced atop the partition that divided the living room and kitchen. My arms issued a grand flourish toward the heavens as I widened my eyes and gazed imperiously down at her.

Using only my voice, gestures, and sky-high perch, I had transformed myself into Endora, the flamboyant witch played by Agnes Moorehead in the TV sitcom *Bewitched*. The show was a huge hit in the 1960s and continued to cast a spell on young viewers like me through its 1970s reruns. To recreate the redheaded sorceress's magical, hovering presence, I'd climbed the living room shelves—carefully keeping my toes away from my mother's treasured blue glass collection—and found the perfect roost. The soaring cathedral ceiling left plenty of room for me to pose dramatically with one skinny leg crossed over the other. With my ringer T-shirt and plain shorts, I didn't have a witch-worthy outfit, but I certainly had the necessary arrogance in my tone.

My mother never batted an eyelash. "Get down from there," she calmly scolded while setting the bags on the dining room table and straightening her polyester shell blouse. "You're going to fall and break your neck." My makeshift Endora then lowered herself with a decided lack of grace, butt-first and splay-legged, onto the top of the giant brown refrigerator in the kitchen before plopping onto the nearby kitchen table. I'd been downgraded to mortal once again.

My mother must have had an inkling back then that I was gay. But the truth is, I didn't know myself. I wasn't even sure what the word "gay" meant. Kids in school used it mostly to describe boys (like me) who sucked at sports and sometimes those (also like me) who walked "like a girl." But we didn't have any references to educate us about issues like sexual orientation and identity. There weren't any positive LGBTQ role models in mass media, and there was no internet to make research easy and shame-free.

Most of my childhood hobbies weren't stereotypically gay or straight. I had no interest in athletics, but I also had no interest in dolls. I was just as much in love with toy cars as I was with outrageous TV witches. With a relatively permissive mother and no siblings around to make fun of my pastimes, I was free to follow my own, judgment-free path, at least within the walls of our maroon, split-level home in western New York State.

Rather than filtering my outsider identity through the lens of Broadway musicals, I tended to interpret the world through the eyes of pop culture, advertising, and corporate branding. I branded various aspects of my life, in fact, in an effort to define and strengthen my self-image, apart from how other kids seemed to see me. I didn't have much fashion sense, but I created the Clothing Rotunda concept to make sure I never repeated the same shirt during any two-week period at school. To combat the taunts I received about the way I walked, I devised an "all-new" way to stroll, with my hips back and my legs jutting forward. I branded the new walk "Front Wheel Drive" and tried it out in the hallways of the middle school. (It didn't go well. Kids asked me if I'd been in an accident.)

The little black-and-white television in my bedroom fed my imagination. One afternoon, I happened to watch *Don't Drink the Water*, a 1969 movie (based on a play by Woody Allen) in which Jackie Gleason and Estelle Parsons portrayed tourists who, while trapped in a fictional Soviet state, traveled around in an ultra-long limousine with diplomatic flags dramatically flying from the front fenders. I didn't care much for the movie (it later got a skimpy thirty-seven percent rating online), but I suddenly realized my life wouldn't be complete until I'd ridden in a limo with flags on it. Just imagine how comfortable those big seats would be, how the ride would be even cushier than my Uncle Ed's chic luxury sedan, and how people would look at us like we were super important. Mom and I would have to wear our most serious faces so everyone would know that we truly belonged in a diplomatic vehicle.

The problem was that we didn't have a limousine. But we did have something that might be upgradeable for my purposes: my mother's brand-new, lipstick-red four-door, which we'd be boarding in just a few days for the 800-mile trip to visit my grandparents in Kentucky. I scavenged the garage (which, together with the basement, was a repository for everything we'd ever owned but no longer used since we seldom threw things away). There, I found two small flags: one patriotically emblazoned with the stars and stripes, and the other with a rather menacing skull and crossbones (hey, you've gotta work with what you've got).

For some indulgent reason, my mother gave me permission to tape the flags to the front fenders of the car. Given her dislike of ostentatiousness, she must have been mortified as she steered her long, flag-graced vehicle out of the driveway, with me sitting regally in the back seat, trying to channel Jackie Gleason and Estelle Parsons. Luckily for my mother, the pirate flag blew off a couple of hours after our departure, as we charged down the interstate like a lost contingent of swashbuckling ambassadors.

Only the stars and stripes still flew as we stopped for lunch, on the second day of our trip, in Leitchfield, a tiny town that sits along the Western Kentucky Parkway. I could barely tear myself away from the latest issue of *Motor Trend* to go into the restaurant. I loved cars even though I wasn't interested in how they worked, and this issue of the magazine was especially fascinating. The main feature was about a woman named Elizabeth Carmichael (whose round face was not unlike my mother's), an automotive executive who, as the head of the Twentieth Century Motor Car Corporation, bilked investors out of millions of dollars while promising to produce an innovative, three-wheeled car called The Dale. The car never happened. But get this: it turned out that Elizabeth Carmichael wasn't born a woman! Back then, the term "transgender" wasn't used, but it was a fascinating story, and I couldn't wait to get to the bottom of it. But that would have to wait. It was lunchtime.

We took a seat at a heavy wooden table near the front window at the diner so I could stare at the cars in the parking lot. A cheery dark-haired waitress approached. She beamed her beautiful smile at both of us and spoke. "What can I get for *you ladies* to drink today?"

Oh my gosh. No.

"I'd like a cola with a lot of ice, please," my mother answered flatly.

My face felt hot as I asked for a drink too.

My mother must have heard that the waitress called us ladies. But why didn't she correct her? Why didn't she say, "Hey, you've made a mistake, lady. That's my son you're talking to!"? Instead, she ordered a Coke. And she didn't say anything to me about it after the waitress walked away, either.

To be fair, I can't blame the server for making the mistake. Sitting there in my ribbed turtleneck and patchwork jeans, with my wavy red hair flowing luxuriously over my ears, I was aiming to make a 1970s fashion statement. I wasn't trying to look like a girl. But when you put unisex fashion on a somewhat effeminate boy with a unisex haircut, you run the risk of being mistaken. Plus, the excess pounds I put on during a bout of middle school mono meant that I could easily have passed as the pudgy daughter of the pudgy woman I'd arrived with. My sassy, modern style was a perfect complement to her conservatively casual look, with her always-practical short haircut and a simple blouse.

Still, the fact that my mother ignored the whole incident made it more embarrassing. So I kept my mouth shut, too, and let our lunchtime conversation stick to the usual travel topics like estimated arrival time and what we'd do at my grandparents' house.

Most likely, the episode was simply the result of my mother's Southern tendency to avoid confrontation at all costs. She may have even thought that drawing attention to the waitress's mistake would have embarrassed me more. But I saw her silence as a sign of shame. I instinctively had never told her when kids called me "faggot" or "gay" in school, and I didn't know if she ever found out that I was verbally bullied or physically threatened. At least I never got into an actual fight, so she never saw me bruised.

The trip continued like any other.

It's no wonder I kept mum after experiencing yet another gender-related situation later that summer. I was enrolled in a day camp that attracted kids from around the Rochester area, mostly from other schools—not the usual group of kids from my town who knew me and my patchwork jeans.

One day after swim class, I realized I'd left my backpack in the swimming pool locker room. I went back just as another group of boys was getting undressed for the next class.

The usual cacophony of early teen banter filled the locker room. Until one boy noticed me. His eyes widened and his mouth opened as big as a victim in a horror movie.

"There's a girl in the boy's locker room!" He shouted.

Everyone turned around. Someone screamed. "Get out!" one boy yelled.

Based on their demeanor, I knew they weren't saying those things to be mean. They really thought I was in the wrong locker room. A mass of unidentifiable faces stared at me as if I'd committed a crime.

I looked down. "I'm not a girl," I mumbled.

I grabbed my bag and turned toward the door. My face burned, and I felt like I needed to go to the bathroom. But I needed to get away as quickly as possible, and I had to be careful not to walk in a girly way. I took studied, careful steps until I was far enough from the locker room so I could sprint to my next class.

As far as I know, no one in my hometown found out about the incident. I never mentioned it to anyone. In my gym classes at Brockport Central School, some boys still called me names because I couldn't catch a football or throw a baseball. But at least they didn't mistake me for an actual girl.

• • •

While my mother's silence in that Leitchfield restaurant fueled my own shame, her relaxed attitude at home provided me with a safe space to be myself. Occasionally, she actively encouraged my quirkiness. Take the Embarrassing Footwear Collection, for example.

No, that wasn't the name of some bizarre new line from your favorite shoe store. It was simply the branding I invented for a fairly common occurrence in our house.

The routine revolved around the mail delivery. "Mark, would you go out and get the mail, please?" my mother would ask in the late morning or early afternoon. She might be washing dishes or cooking or typing something in her bedroom, or just lying on the couch.

"I don't have my shoes on," I'd answer lazily, trying to avoid even the simplest of chores.

"Here," she'd respond, slipping off her tan, imitation leather low-rise mules. "Put these on and just run across the road. It'll only take you five seconds."

I always accepted the invitation. I considered it an exciting challenge. Sliding my feet into her shoes from Ames, a discount department store chain that at one time was one of the nation's biggest discount retailers, I'd bound out of the front door and across the yard that I probably should have mowed days before, clenching my toes to hold the gawky footwear in place as I darted across the road to the mailbox. I wondered what passing drivers might think of a skinny teenage boy running around in overly comfortable women's wear (or maybe they just thought I was a girl). But it didn't matter. My mother was with me on this one.

12. Charm Offensive

New York City, September 2015

Leaving your mother in a nursing home means putting her in the hands of people you don't know. And while I had no specific reasons to worry about my mother's treatment, I wanted to make darn sure that the staff liked her—and me. I pondered every interaction I had with the employees, wondering if it would have a positive or negative effect. Would they be mean to my mother if I annoyed them? Would they treat her better if I charmed them?

My charm offensive was multi-pronged. I eagerly chatted up every staff member that I could. In the nicest and most naturally conversational tones, I found out where they were from and where they lived, jotting every staff member's name and details in a blue notebook that my mother had once used to take notes for the local history books that she wrote. If anyone had ever found that notebook, they would have thought I was stalking the entire care team.

I empathized with the staff whenever I could. Bad subway commute to work? Putting in long hours on a Saturday? Oh gee, I could certainly relate to any complaints. If an employee hailed from a place I'd visited, I'd gush about how much I loved their country. Being a travel writer enabled me to talk details with a wide variety of people.

My campaign was gradual, ongoing, and repetitive—a combination of high-stakes relationship-building paired with the "lather, rinse, repeat" frequency of the finest dandruff shampoo. It also drew some inspiration from hostage negotiation tactics.

My strategy kicked in every time the elevator doors parted on the second floor of the nursing home, as a smile spread across my face to charm the head nurses at the main desk.

The nurses always smiled back; they were consistently friendly and competent. But their time was thinly spread, and I knew they simply couldn't pay much attention to any one patient for very long.

The more crucial interactions took place once I proceeded down the slippery-clean hallway, where I'd greet the nurse's aides—the women we relied on for everything from dressing my mother to taking her to the bathroom to giving her food. I couldn't imagine how much suffering they'd seen, how much poop they'd wiped, how much death they'd witnessed. But most of the aides still managed to smile and say hello when I passed them.

Tina stopped me one day as I walked away from her desk. "Your mother is still in physical therapy this morning. She should be done in just a few minutes if you want to go pick her up. She's in the rehab clinic on the first floor."

My mother had done some major damage to one hand and arm when she fell at her previous residence, and she still required physical therapy. Upon arrival at Venerable Hills, she'd been restricted to a wheelchair—not because she was too weak to stand on her own, but because she was too confused and unable to prevent herself from falling. She didn't recognize her own limitations.

According to nursing home policy, only a nurse or an aide could provide physical assistance. Visitors weren't allowed to help residents get in or out of wheelchairs, bed, or the bathroom, even if they were family. If she needed to use the toilet or move between bed and chair, I had to call for a staff member. And for all the times that I wasn't there, well, I just hoped she could grab someone's attention or ring the buzzer that hung next to the bed and make her needs known. She never complained about having to wait for attention—maybe because she never had to. Or maybe she just couldn't remember.

· · ·

I felt like a parent picking up a kid as I peered through the window of the rehab clinic. The din of exercise machines filled the air as I opened the door of the spacious facility, which was larger than any other room I'd seen at this facility. Therapists and patients worked with various contraptions in every corner, pushing and pulling, stretching and flexing with a variety of clicks and whirs.

And there was my mother, in her wheelchair, holding the world's tiniest dumbbell in her bum hand. The sleeves of her pink ribbed sweater were rolled up a bit to allow for greater flexibility, emphasizing how slim her arms had gotten in recent months. She gazed intently at her own hand through tinted eyeglasses, as if she might be able to move the dumbbell through telekinesis. She was dressed in now-oversized dark blue polyester pants that dated to the time when she was slightly overweight, complemented by slip-on shoes that my husband Angel had bought for her when her feet started swelling. Her short waves of brown and gray hair were neater than usual, indicating that someone had probably combed it more attentively this morning.

A handsome young man in a lab coat stood by her side, his hand resting on her arm. I approached and introduced myself. His name was Francisco.

"Your mother is really making progress. Aren't you, Mrs. Chesnut?" he smiled broadly as he put his hand on her shoulder. His brilliant smile glistened as much as his neat, jet-black hair.

She patted his hand. "Well, I'm just an old woman, but I do what I can." It was cute to see her act like this in conversation with a man; she'd never dated after my father died (as far as I know), and I'd never even seen her flirt. When I asked her once why she never considered remarrying, she said, "I never wanted to run the risk of someone being mean to you."

I thanked Francisco for his attention and grasped the handles of the wheelchair, rolling my mother down the hall.

"I honestly don't see the point of therapy, but at least it's something to do," she said as the elevator ascended. "It beats sitting around staring at the wall."

Francisco's smile was one of the brightest that I'd seen at the nursing home. But it was almost equaled by the staff member we ran into on the second floor.

"Hello, mama, how are you?" the stout woman in floral medical garb said, beaming as she leaned forward to touch my mother's arm. "You doing okay?"

It was Roseline, my favorite nurse's aide. I loved that she always called my mother "mama," and I appreciated her gentleness whenever she helped her to the bathroom or dining room. Roseline and I had bonded over our shared affection for the Caribbean island she called home; I'd been there on a press trip and its historic sites and natural beauty impressed me.

My mother and I stopped in the library, a lounge with one row of bookshelves that housed a diverse collection of titles, just steps from the occasional beeps of the nursing station. I rolled her up to inspect a wall of tomes that ranged from trashy novels to coffee table books and World War II nostalgia. I never saw anyone actually looking at anything in the library; people went there more to make use of the couch, the cozy armchairs, and the table.

Sometimes, just to engage her and make conversation, I'd pull out a book or two and ask her what she thought about the cover illustration. Today, I tried to get a rise out of her. I pulled out a sappy romance novel by her least-favorite author.

Back in Brockport, she spat out a condescending comment about "trash" when she saw an entire section of that writer's books in the library of her assisted living facility. But this time, she just smiled and said, "Oh no, I don't think I'd like that one." And that was it.

I took a seat in a soft, high-backed armchair and changed the subject.

"Roseline is so nice, isn't she?" I said.

"Most of the people here are okay," my mother responded, looking around the room. She leaned toward me, raising her bandaged hand to the side of her mouth as she whispered, "but *that* woman is a bitch." She pointed a crooked finger, and I immediately knew who she was talking about.

I turned and there she was: Beatrice, a corpulent aide with a wide gait and misleadingly cheerful medical smock, slowly pushing a giant maintenance cart down the hall. She was the one staff member who had never regaled me with a smile. I sensed her unhappiness. During various interactions, I'd also noticed how, even though she knew my mother was confused and hard of hearing, Beatrice never attempted to speak slower or louder. I think I'd only heard my mother use the word "bitch" about three times in my life, so the fact that she used it on Beatrice made me worry that the aide might be worse than I thought.

"I'd say something to her about how I'm paying a lot of money to be here and I'm paying her salary, but she'd probably toss me around, just to show who's boss," my mother added.

"Has she ever hurt you?" I asked quietly, thankful that Beatrice was walking farther down the hall.

"No, but I wouldn't put it past her."

What could I do? Report Beatrice for being a bitch? It might make matters worse if I angered the staff without having a concrete complaint.

With no other recourse, I redoubled my charm offensive with her.

"Thanks so much, Beatrice," I gushed the next day when she plopped a pitcher of water on a tray in my mother's room. "How's your day going?"

"It's going okay," she said as she emptied the plastic waste-basket that belonged to my mother's roommate.

"I heard the trains were a mess today," I said. "Did it take you long to get here?"

"There were delays on the E train. But I still made it on time."

My mother, who was relaxing in bed, silently sipped her cup of water and looked at the muted talk show on her wall-mounted TV. I squeezed her hand.

"Oh, you live in Queens?" I asked Beatrice.

"Yes, I do."

"Me too. I live in Jackson Heights."

She wiped off a side table without looking up.

"You gonna need more water?" she asked, lumbering over to my mother's bedside. "You want me to change you?"

"I'm sorry, I can't hear well," my mother said, smiling and touching her own ear.

"You gonna need more water? You want me to change you?" Same speed. Same tone. My mother looked at me to translate.

"She's asking if you'd like some more water, Momma. And if you need to go to the bathroom."

"Oh, no. I'm fine. Thank you." My mother nodded with the artificially polite smile she always used to shorten uncomfortable conversations. It reminded me of how she acted when I was growing up if a crazy person approached us on the street when we visited big cities like Rochester or Louisville.

Beatrice turned and plodded away. "I guarantee she'll be complaining about going to the bathroom as soon as I leave," she mumbled. I knew that, thankfully, my mother didn't hear that last comment.

"What's her name again?" my mother whispered, pointing toward the door. She still couldn't remember the name of a single staff member.

"Beatrice."

"Oh. Well, I'm glad she's gone."

"She's a real charmer," I answered, patting her hand and realizing I didn't recognize the floral-patterned, short-sleeved blouse that my mother wore. I put my arm around her shoulder and discreetly looked at the sewn-on nametag that was required on all the residents' clothing. Instead of Eunice Chesnut, it had the name of a woman I didn't know. The blouse wasn't my mother's. But I made the executive decision to not complain about it. At least she was wearing clean clothes every day. I was also pretty sure I'd be dealing with Beatrice again in the future, so I had to choose my battles.

"So ... how did physical therapy go this morning, Momma?"

"Very well," she said. "Did you go to my class? That Francisco is a *very* nice young man."

Wow. This was the first time she'd remembered someone's name at the nursing home. I guess I didn't need to use my charm offensive on him.

13. Eunice's Tips for Top-Flight Air Travel

1. Don't drive yourself to the airport. Long-term parking is expensive, so ask a friend to drop you off—but ask a different friend to pick you up. That way you only inconvenience each person once.

2. Always arrive at the airport a solid hour before domestic departures. If you're flying international, make it two hours. It's better to have time to kill at the airport rather than to feel rushed by running late. (Plus, that way your son will have more time to wander around the airport since that seems to be the only thing he ever wants to do.)

3. Stay physically connected to your belongings at all times in the airport. One hand should be on your bag when you're sitting down, or else wrap a strap around your arm or leg. That way you'll notice if someone tries to take it and you can scream bloody murder.

4. When you're on the plane and see the beverage cart coming, make your desire crystal clear. Slam down that table tray as fast as you possibly can and rest your hands firmly on top. Do not fall asleep. Do not watch a movie. Don't take your eyes off the cart until they've served you. You don't want to miss out on the free pop and peanuts, do you?

5. Always bring something to read and something to snack on. Plastic-wrapped, bright orange peanut butter crackers are the best option because the peanut butter has some nutritional value and they never go bad since the crackers have so many chemicals. You never know when you might be hungry and stranded, with no access to food.

14. Arrivals and Departures

Chicago O'Hare International Airport, 1977

I watched a man die at gate K2 at O'Hare Airport. Or at least I think I did. He collapsed on the floor and belched a clear liquid that ran all over his face and onto his suit and tie. Then he went stiff. Onlookers set down their luggage and pressed their hands to their mouths. It looked like a slow-motion live-art exhibit, a dramatic contrast to the fast-walking travelers charging past the gate, oblivious to what was happening. After a few minutes, three serious-faced men wearing oversized coats rushed in with a stretcher and knelt around the man.

I wanted to see if the guy would start moving again or if he was really dead. But I needed to get back to my own gate, where my mother and a green-striped Ozark Air Lines DC-9 waited. Mom would be mad if we missed the flight to St. Louis because then we'd miss our next connection to Paducah.

Watching someone die should have scared me when I was that age. But in my adolescent mind, the incident at gate K2 was just part of the excitement of living a jet-set life. Seeing someone die in your everyday life would be frightening, for sure. But death was another experience entirely, I reasoned, when there was a snow-covered jet parked just outside, ready to whisk travelers off to some impossibly exotic destination.

Our warm-weather road trips to see my grandparents in Kentucky were exciting. But they couldn't hold a candle to our Christmas visits, when the possibility of blizzards always prompted my mother to book airline tickets. And I was able to witness the medical drama playing out at gate K2 because, for the past couple of years, Mom had let me wander the airport terminals alone during long layovers, while she stayed put at the gate and read a book.

I slowly made my way back down the concourse, my skin bristling beneath my green striped turtleneck every time an open jetway door spewed a frigid blast into the otherwise overheated terminal. A medley of tinny announcements, distant background music, and the rapid-fire click-clicks of departure-gate keyboards filled the air as I studied the people sitting at each gate.

I spotted important-looking businessmen with decidedly grown-up briefcases. Well-dressed women with shiny purses that matched their high-heeled pumps. And sometimes entire families carrying matching tote bags with airline logos (I would have killed to have a bag like that). The airport was a showcase of more diverse clothing styles, hairdos, races, and ethnicities than I'd seen anywhere else—even at Midtown Plaza in Rochester, which was the nation's first urban indoor shopping center when it opened in 1961.

These travelers at O'Hare had things to do, places to go. No one on the concourse knew I lived in the only house in my neighborhood with a gravel driveway. No one noticed that I walked like a girl. The flight attendants, who strutted down the concourse with the utmost of style, didn't care if I couldn't throw a baseball. When we flew, we were simply—and elegantly—*passengers*.

I was fascinated by the unique vocabulary of air travel, which bestows travelers with a temporary title much more exciting than any designation that a degree or a royal appointment might provide. Listen to the announcements in the airport. If they're looking for you, you're no longer Mr. or Mrs. Smith.

You're *Passenger Smith*. I fantasized that someday I might be worthy enough to hear my own name thundering through the din of a busy terminal. "Passenger Chesnut, please pick up the red airport courtesy phone for a message."

I also loved the airline industry's term for garbage, which magically becomes "all remaining service items." If you just pass your trash to the flight attendant, she'll make it all disappear, just like she can make your troubles at home disappear with a few simple words: prepare for departure.

Considering my annual airline trips (and less frequent trips to Florida and Arizona) an integral part of my identity, I visually documented every flight. I kept a personal route map at home, on which I carefully drew every new route that I might fly. Personal route maps say something about who we are and what's important to us. They are unique, and they are permanent. You could lose just about everything in life: your money, your job, your relationship. But no one can take away the memories of the places you've visited. Your personal route map is indestructible.

I knew that my mother and I weren't as glamorous as most travelers. Real globetrotters, of course, didn't have a thirteen-year-old kid in tow like my mother did, and they weren't taking three planes just to land in Paducah, Kentucky (not to say that Paducah wasn't glamorous; it was a stop on Joan Crawford's bottling plant tour and the one-time home of Lily Tomlin's parents, after all. It's also one of only two cities mentioned in the song "Hooray for Hollywood." But still, Paris it's not—although it is bigger than Paris, Tennessee).

Indeed, the truly elite sipped champagne and sliced into thick steaks in first-class cabins bound for distant places like London and Hong Kong. But I didn't care about the destination. I was convinced that excitement awaited everywhere, even in the lesser-known cities on the route maps of regional carriers like North Central Airlines and Southern Airways. For a boy who just wanted to escape, any flight provided relief from the voices back at school and the stresses of gym class.

I gazed at the gigantic departure board, which hung so high that people had to crane their necks as if it were a high-tech sign from heaven. Numbers and letters ticked and whirred with every arrival and departure as I pondered the foreign-sounding allure of cities like Eau Claire, Pierre, and Marquette. I speculated about the difference between Sioux Falls and Sioux City. And I was especially intrigued by exotic, multi-city destinations like Wausau/Stevens Point, Marion/Herrin, and Cape Girardeau/Sikeston. Any place that's important enough to have two names must be pretty darn cool.

And then there was the conglomeration destination of not just two, not even three, but four places: the Quad Cities. The destination had a mysterious air, actually. Why did the airlines never announce the actual names of those four cities? Could anyone even name all of them? I knew I couldn't. But if I could someday visit, even for a few days, my life would surely be much more fascinating.

I grabbed thick airline timetables from a couple of check-in counters before hustling over to the Ozark Air Lines gates, which were furnished with spectacularly bright, curved plastic seats. A vibrant poster flaunted the soaring beauty of the St. Louis Arch, the airline's slogan promising that if only you'd fly Ozark, they'd "make it easy for you." What exactly that meant was as much a mystery to me as the names of the four Quad Cities.

My mother slid a thick novel into her giant brown purse, which didn't quite match her sensible, low-heeled sling-back sandals. Her look couldn't compete with the fashion statements I'd seen on the bigger concourse where the more international airlines docked, but at least she was color-coordinated, right down to her sensibly cut brown hair.

"I just saw a dead guy!" I eagerly called out as I approached.

"Shhhh … you can tell me about that later," she answered as she pulled out our boarding passes. "I'm trying to listen to the announcement about our flight."

I gazed out at the plane that we would soon board, admiring the logo on the tail, an abstract representation of three swallows flying through a green swirl. In a matter of minutes, I'd once again be inhaling the potent aroma of jet fuel in the cold winter air and feeling the welcoming caress of the cloth airline seats. I was going somewhere.

15. Institutional Living

New York City, September 2015

My mother wore a faint smile as she gazed out the picture window at a plane fading into the distance. The aircraft gently tilted its wings back and forth as if waving goodbye before shrinking into the cloudless blue sky.

In years past, we'd watched planes from airport departure gates before embarking on our own adventures. Now, we observed the jet-fueled action from behind the walls of a nursing home.

"Do you remember when we used to fly to Kentucky to see Pop and Gran for Christmas?" I asked, kneeling next to my mother's wheelchair. The facility's top-floor lounge had become a favored stop during my visits because of the view it offered of the Manhattan skyline as well as the flights departing from nearby LaGuardia Airport. The visuals gave us something to talk about.

"Oh yes, I think I remember that," she responded, resting her good hand on the one that was bandaged. "We always had a good time traveling together, didn't we?" The fact that she didn't say anything more specific indicated that she probably didn't recall much about our trips. But that was okay. What mattered was that we were talking. Her eyes sparkled and she looked pretty in her now too-big pink sweater. Her tousled hair was getting longer, and she'd need a haircut soon, but overall she looked pretty good.

I pushed her slowly down a glistening hall lined with medical and cleaning equipment. As we passed various residents and staff members, my mother started her usual smile-wave-and-greet routine with anyone who looked her way.

"Most people here aren't very friendly," she said as we reached the end of the corridor. "But I always try to say hello."

As we exited the elevator on the second floor, she surprised me with a request.

"Stop for just a minute, honey, I want to introduce you to my *one real friend* here," she said, pointing to a bleach-blonde woman standing at the reception desk, one hand casually resting on a walker. Her hairstyle and neatly applied makeup were a vague reimagining of an older Lana Turner.

My mother reached out to her. "This is my good friend ..." she said, stopping in mid-sentence, her mouth open as she began to chuckle. "Well, now I can't remember your name, *friend!*"

"I'm Mary." The woman smiled back, touching my mother's hand. "It's good to see you, Eunice. This must be your son!"

Our encounter with Mary was astonishing; this was the first time my mother had introduced me to *anyone* since moving into the nursing home, and the first time she'd described someone there as a friend. My mother was hard of hearing and the tumor was erasing her short-term memory. She often didn't recognize staff or fellow residents and couldn't remember anyone's names, except for family members and her handsome young physical therapist (finally, my mother and I had similar taste in men). So the fact that she wanted me to meet her "one real friend" was indeed touching.

Seeing my mother socializing also assuaged some of the guilt I'd been feeling about my nearly two-week absence due to an extended work trip that took me to Mexico, Panama, and Peru. I had stopped traveling completely for a couple of months after her arrival, but since I was a travel writer, remaining stationary wasn't sustainable for long. Both my hubby and my sister had encouraged me to take this trip, especially since it was important from a career perspective. I'd be speaking at two conferences and consulting with a tour operator to help create new vacation packages.

I think it was my sister who used in-flight emergency instructions as an analogy for the need to pay attention to your own needs as well as those of your aging parent: should there be a loss in cabin pressure, you must put on your own mask before helping anyone next to you. You're no use to anyone else if you're passed out—or wiped out from exhaustion at Venerable Hills. During my absence, Angel visited my mother several times a week and my sister traveled from New Jersey every weekend. I still felt bad. But it was better if Momma had found a neighbor to talk to when there were no visitors around.

With her easy conversational style and wheelchair-free mobility, Mary seemed to be in far better shape than most second-floor residents, both physically and mentally.

I read somewhere that dementia and stroke are the most common chronic medical conditions in nursing home residents, and a sizeable percentage have mental disorders. If you took a stroll through the second floor where my mother lived on any random day, you'd quickly realize the accuracy of those statistics. My mother wasn't the only one who had trouble making friends, and everyday conversations were few and far between for most residents. The television may have blared in the lounge, the medical devices may have clanged, but the people living there were usually silent. Most had no visitors. Ever. Whenever I was there—no matter the day or hour—nearly everyone would be sitting alone, wheelchair-bound, in their room or one of the three lounges.

The facility offered an extensive schedule of live entertainment in the form of music, karaoke sing-alongs, book readings, and games, but most residents had limited ability to participate and mingle. Those who could socialize were eager to find conversational partners, and I tried to chat them up whenever I could. I felt powerless to improve their situation. I could barely lift my own mother's mood. But still, I chatted.

• • •

Institutional living comes in many forms. More than seventy years earlier, my father spent nearly two years as an unwilling guest at Stalag Luft I, a prisoner-of-war camp on Germany's Baltic coast, after Nazis shot down his B-17 Flying Fortress over the Netherlands.

He died of cancer when I was four, so I was too young to ask him about his experiences. But my mother said he barely spoke about his time as a prisoner. She later shared a few memories during an interview for a local history project. "The one thing he did say was, 'We were hungry all the time, but we weren't starving the way the prisoners in the Japanese camps were. Sometimes we were lucky and got bread, but there was nothing to go with it. It was dry, stale, and often had bugs in it. But we ate it anyway.'" His six-foot frame grew gaunt, and he looked sick by the time the war ended.

The letters he wrote from the camp, which were closely monitored and subject to censorship by his captors, recounted mundane activities like smoking cigarettes and reading books. My mother had stored nearly all his correspondence in a giant box in the utility room of her house, and now the collection of yellowed missives sat in my apartment.

"This afternoon I went to a variety show, which was put on by the Americans and was intended to represent a typical two-hour period of radio programs," he wrote to his parents in April 1944. "It was, therefore, made up of singing, a serial story, a dance orchestra, and several commercials. The orchestra was especially good, since some of its members once played in big bands in America."

With Nazis reviewing his every word, there were no mentions of bugs in the bread.

Years later, I got another glimpse of institutional life while visiting leprosy settlements.

During the late nineteenth century, thousands of people around the globe contracted leprosy, and many who tested positive were permanently exiled to isolated facilities. You might be tempted to call those sites "leper colonies," but don't. The word "leper" is considered offensive, since it hearkens to biblical times when the disease was viewed as God's punishment. The modern name for the condition is Hansen's Disease.

The United States operated a surprisingly far-flung network of these settlements. Some still operate today, although technically the few residents who live there now are no longer patients, since Hansen's Disease is treatable on an outpatient basis. These people stayed because—well, think about it. If you've spent most of your life forcibly sequestered from society, you weren't allowed to work or socialize in the outside world and you're already a senior citizen, where are you going to go?

I discovered that several of these facilities still existed, in one form or another, and my professional fascination led me to visit, write about, and photograph sites in Hawaii, Louisiana, South Africa, and Panama, where I interviewed residents about their life experiences.

Some of my longest conversations took place at Palo Seco, a Hansen's Disease settlement that the US government opened in the Panama Canal Zone in 1907. Beneath swaying palm trees just steps from a rocky beach, I met a woman in her eighties who'd spent more than five decades at the facility. Her world had changed when she received the leprosy diagnosis at age eighteen. Suddenly, plans to marry her boyfriend were cancelled as government health officials shuttled her off to the new US-run treatment facility, set along an otherwise unspoiled stretch of Atlantic coastline. Eventually, she fell in love with another patient and married him, and I met them both during my two visits.

During one of our meetings, which took place in a wood-framed cafeteria that looked out on the Pacific Ocean, she told me that the secret to happiness is to have faith and patience. Her husband concurred, saying you need to be able to accept things as they are, nothing more.

• • •

As a college student, I loved living away from home but hated the institutional aspect of living on a university campus. Dormitories are, ideally, happier places than most institutions, to be sure. But that didn't keep me from whining about the controlled aspects of campus life, from the uniformly furnished rooms to the predetermined cafeteria meals and regimented schedules. Still, I had no problem overlooking those negatives to make friends, get drunk, eat pizza, and get an education.

Leprosy settlements, prisoner-of-war camps, and college campuses are vastly different settings. What they have in common is that, in many cases, the patients, prisoners, and students can turn to each other—and perhaps visitors—for social and emotional support. They can assess their own situation and find inner strength. Most nursing home residents, at least in my experience, can't, and most don't have families or friends who visit and provide emotional support. The human connection is weak or nonexistent.

• • •

After spending a few minutes with Mary, my mother and I moved farther down the hall, where a short, stout woman with a Catholic school gym teacher's haircut raised her arm toward us as if she was a crossing guard who took her job a bit too seriously. I already knew that this was Betty, a resident who always looked like she was about to jump out of her wheelchair and slug someone. We obeyed her signal and dutifully stopped by her side.

"Hey, did I ever tell you about the time I was trapped in my shower at home?" she asked.

"No, I don't think so," I responded.

"Well, let me tell you, it was the worst," Betty said, her thick New York City accent twisting the last word. "I was all by myself because my jackass ex-husband had just left me. I was taking a shower and I passed out in the stall. It was one of those freestanding shower stalls with a door. When I woke up, I couldn't get the damned door open. I was too weak."

"Oh, that's awful!"

"You *bet your ass* it was awful. Trapped, right in my own shower! I was so weak that I finally had to tear off the entire side of the shower stall. Kicking and punching until it fell. It was the only way I could get out."

My mother smiled and nodded as I congratulated Betty on her great escape. I wondered how a woman who was too weak to open a flimsy door could be strong enough to destroy the entire side of a stall. Perhaps superhuman strength only works in certain directions.

"She's very chatty, isn't she?" my mother said once we arrived at the sunroom, grinning as she dug into a fresh bag of potato chips. "I try to be friendly with her, but she'll just talk, talk, talk, and sometimes I don't have the faintest idea what she's talking about."

It wasn't long before vaguely culinary aromas announced the arrival of dinner time. Guests technically weren't allowed in the dining room during meal time, but the staff always let me roll my mother to her place at one of the four-person tables, each of which was covered with a disposable tablecloth.

I was pleased when a nurse's aide said to put my mother at a table with Mary and a pleasant-looking redheaded woman who I hadn't met, but who seemed happy to converse.

"I've been living in Jackson Heights for more than forty years," the redhead proudly told me, her chin raised. The scent of ham entered the dining room.

"That's wonderful!" I said. "I've been here for a few years, and I love it."

"I used to love it too." Her face suddenly scowled, extra wrinkles growing around her tense lips. Her fake red hair suddenly seemed redder. "But then the foreigners came. *Those people*, they come here from other countries and they ruin everything."

"Oh, are you from originally from New York?" I asked.

"No. I'm from Ireland."

"Ohhh, well ..." *I guess she thinks some foreigners are better than others.*

Suddenly I decided that my mother required my immediate attention, and I dropped the conversation mid-sentence. I squatted down to say goodbye.

"You're always so good at talking to people," she said, touching my hand on the wheelchair's armrest. "I've always said you're a great conversationalist and you talk to everyone about where they're from." She didn't seem to remember that she was the one who'd taught me those skills, through years of training at church and social events.

She squeezed my hand tighter and her voice lowered. "But I don't want you to talk to any of these people for too long," she whispered, "because it cuts into our time together."

16. The Votes Are In

Brockport, 1977

I found a place to hide, crouching behind a parked car and holding my breath to stifle any blubbering that might give away my location.

The footsteps were getting closer on the dark pavement, accompanied by a smoker's labored breathing. The faint smell of liquor tickled my nostrils.

I wiped tears from my face as my eyed darted around the parking lot for an escape route. There was none. My safest bet was to stay put and be very, very quiet. I stared down at the shiny brown shoes my mother had bought me for the first day of seventh grade and tried to make myself smaller as I grasped the grooves of the rubber tire.

"Mark, where are you?" the woman's gruff voice slurred. "Come here, honey, I want to talk to you!"

I peered under the car and saw a pair of imitation leather sling-back pumps near the exhaust pipe. I froze, sobbing silently.

The pumps turned and walked away.

I hope nobody saw me crying.

My mother had just lost her bid to become town clerk of Sweden, the western New York town that was home to the village of Brockport. Most people—including my mother—

graciously accept losses in the company of supportive colleagues. I, however, faced defeat by huddling against a cold tire in a parking lot.

. . .

Being a politician had never been a goal for fifty-something Eunice Chesnut. But she had made lots of friends through volunteer activities at a variety of organizations, including the Sweden Democratic Party, where she'd worked on the local campaigns of George McGovern and Jimmy Carter. The Democrats—who were a tiny minority in the conservative town of Sweden—took note of her extensive social network and invited her to run for office. She thought it would be an interesting experience for herself as well as for me.

I put all the energy that a seventh grader could muster into the campaign. I canvassed the town with my mother, shook hands, distributed flyers, and gave bumper stickers to the teachers in my school who I knew were Democrats thanks to the voter registration list that party organizers gave us.

Learning the political affiliations of every person in town kind of went against some of my mother's parenting precepts. She wanted me to judge people based on who they were, not on labels that could be applied to them. She'd always been friends with people of every stripe, and she avoided telling me about their political, religious, or ethnic backgrounds. Her Southern upbringing placed religion, race, and politics firmly in the realm of topics to avoid. But in this case, I guess she felt it was worth the risk of exposing me to a trove of personal political data if it meant that I could learn something about democracy.

"Now remember, we know we're not going to win," my mother had warned as she steered her bright red sedan toward the election night party at the VFW club lodge. Her short, wavy hair was combed into its signature practical style and she was decked out in the same plus-sized, multicolored pantsuit that she'd worn in her official campaign headshot. I sported equally multicolored corduroy pants and a turtleneck that I hoped would make the best possible fashion statement.

"I know, I know, Mom."

"It's good to give people choices. And it's been a fun experience, hasn't it?"

"Yeah, it's been cool."

I loved campaigning, watching my mother act like the politicians you see on TV and seeing the word CHESNUT—a surname that invited mockery from schoolkids and annoying misspellings by grown-ups—emblazoned (and spelled correctly) on signs and bumper stickers around town.

A sea of smiling faces greeted us as we entered the wood-paneled clubhouse, a rag-tag facility used for everything from poker nights to budget-friendly wedding receptions. Debby Boone's ditty "You Light Up My Life" oozed from some distant speaker as we made our way through the crowd, my mother beaming and throwing out witty one-liners about her impending loss as I shook men's hands just like my mother had taught me to do at church.

Over in the corner, behind overflowing bowls of potato chips and pretzels, a group of teenagers—children of the candidates and party volunteers—hung out. Most of them were a year or two older than me. They looked like the cast of a movie about cool kids. There was the muscular jock, the handsome smart boy, and the pretty girl with long blonde hair and a stellar reputation. They surely had been too busy and popular to have bothered working on their parents' nerdy political campaigns.

I, on the other hand, had the dubious honor of being the only kid regularly involved in the election efforts. The grown-ups had trusted me with critical tasks like greeting people and handing out material, and sometimes they'd even asked my opinion about strategies. I felt comfortable with them. Growing up as an only (in practice) child, I had always spent a lot of time in the company of my mother's friends. I was still trying to develop the social skills needed to navigate the world of peers my own age.

There was nothing I wanted less than to go anywhere near that group of kids in the corner of the clubhouse.

"Go get yourself some snacks and something to drink," my mother said. "And can you please bring me a pop, with lots of ice?"

Crap.

I walked over to the snack table and looked up at the kids, all of whom were taller than me. Andy Gibb was crooning "I Just Want to Be Your Everything" in the background.

"Hi," I said softly as I reached for a giant bottle of soda pop.

"Hi Mark," the long-haired girl said. The other kids glanced at me, smiled, and turned away. These weren't the bullies at school who called me names or threatened to beat me up. These kids were actually scarier. They were polite, normal teenagers who were socially adept and had vibrant social lives. Their parents were friends with my mother, and we were all in the same party, both politically and at this moment in the lodge. These were the kids I most wanted to impress. Or, at the very least, convince that I wasn't a loser. Lacking the faintest clue about what to say next, I inserted several pretzel twists into my mouth so that I wouldn't be able to speak if anyone else talked to me.

I'd finished chewing by the time I got back to my mother's table. I was back in my element, with adults I called by their first names and easily manageable topics that ranged from local real estate developments to the newest stores at Brockport Plaza to the proposed left-turn lane on Main Street. Would it really improve the traffic situation? Oh my word, we'll really feel like a big city if we get that extra lane!

Eventually, a volunteer stood up with a marker in his hand. The music shut off as the vote counts from each district started trickling in. Everyone stood up as he began scrawling the results on a giant poster board.

Each number was worse than the one before. The mood was still jovial, though, since no one expected to win. The candidates started grouping together to talk, and I found myself standing alone. I went to get a drink as increasingly poor numbers kept appearing on the board. I suddenly felt a tear welling in my eye as I realized that my mother was losing, and badly.

It's okay. This isn't a surprise. I can be cool. She's actually doing better than any Democrat has ever done in a local race. So just be cool.

This was it. The CHESNUT signs would tumble from people's yards. The bumper stickers would be scraped off cars. My mother's face would no longer appear on the front page of the *Brockport Post*. We weren't going to be like Jimmy Carter's family. We'd be like George McGovern's.

The cool kids were still standing near the table. Their parents had lost too, but they probably didn't care that much. They were too busy hanging out and talking about things like sports and dating.

I hadn't noticed that Tanya, a campaign volunteer, was ambling her way to the snack table. She wore the uneven grin of a woman who'd hit the sauce long before the polls closed.

"Hey Mark, what's wrong?" she slurred, inspecting my face with squinted eyes that accentuated her smudged eyeliner. "You see the election results? I'm sorry about your mom."

"Yeah, I saw," I mumbled, smiling artificially as I turned to walk away.

Tanya grabbed my arm as a potent blend of cologne and alcohol engulfed me. "You did a really good job helping her, sweetie," she drawled.

The cool kids were watching us, smiling slightly. Suddenly my sweater felt prickly.

Don't cry, don't cry.

My lips trembled. My breath suddenly heaved as tears slowly streamed down my cheeks.

Yanking my arm from Tanya's tight grip, I made a dash to the nearest door and out onto the dark lawn. Well, it wasn't exactly a dash. That would have attracted too much attention. It must have been a fast-paced stride, my legs so close together that my butt teeter-tottered like a well-dressed secretary in a Rock Hudson movie.

The booze must have bestowed Tanya with superhuman powers because she seemed to arrive outside before I did. I ran toward the parking lot and, happily, found refuge behind a giant Oldsmobile.

I just wanted to be alone. I didn't want a drunk lady shining a spotlight on me, especially in front of the cool kids. The parking lot provided a refuge. And I'd finally outsmarted Tanya. She was walking away.

I stood up and watched her stumble back into the clubhouse. I stayed outside for about forty-five minutes, staring at automobiles, until my mother came out.

"Okay sweetie, let's go," she said.

The car was quiet as she steered us toward home. "I couldn't find you inside, so I'm not sure if you saw that everyone lost," she said quietly. "But just remember we did the best we could, and you were a big help. We knew we weren't going to win."

"I know."

"Are you hungry? Do you want to stop at the drive-through?"

"Okay."

For the next couple weeks, I stayed extra alert at school, so I could walk the other way if I saw one of the cool Democratic kids in the hallway. On Thursday, the long-haired girl walked right past me. I don't know if she saw me or not, but she didn't say anything. It was the same as before. Political landscapes don't shift easily.

17. Taking It on the Chin

The idea of plucking my mother's chin grossed me out.

She'd been rubbing her face as we chatted, using her left hand since the right one was still tethered to a brace and wrapped in a thick bandage. My husband Angel and I sat on the pleasantly upholstered sofa in the nursing home's library. It was a typical Saturday afternoon visit with my mother. Then the request came.

"Do you think you could do me a favor, sweetie?" she said. "I've got some whiskers right here, and they're really bothering me. But I can't get them out with my hand all tied up like this." More than two months had passed, and she hadn't fully recovered from the fall that precipitated her move to New York City. The fact that she was wheelchair-bound didn't seem to bother her as much as her inability to perform basic tasks with her right hand.

"Um, I don't know, Momma," I said, smiling nervously while patting the sleeve of the purple sweater that cradled her shrinking frame. "I've never plucked anyone's chin before, and I don't want to hurt you."

Oh, no, no, no. I cannot do this.

I'd never removed a hair from anyone, not even from my own body, so the idea of forcibly yanking anything from my mother's frail face terrified me. What if she passed out from the pain? What if the jolt triggered a cascading series of reactions, causing some bizarre sort of hair follicle seizure that would in turn spark an extreme conniption and violent, sudden death, leaving me perched guiltily on the couch, trying to explain to the staff why I had simultaneously killed my mother and littered the floor with random facial hair?

Plus, there was the intimacy issue. The bond between mother and son is strong, and perhaps even more so when it's a two-person household and the son is gay. That's a lot of togetherness.

I guess that's why one scene in the 1974 Martin Scorsese film *Alice Doesn't Live Here Anymore* weirded me out when I was growing up. In many ways, the film was the decade's most relatable Hollywood depiction of a widowed mother-and-son relationship. But in one scene, the mother, played by Ellen Burstyn, removes a drinking straw from a fast-food cup and playfully flicks soda at her son, initiating a minor playfight. To me, that was something only friends, siblings, or romantic partners would do (not that I had any of the three with whom to test my theory). A mother shouldn't act in such a casual and physical way with her son. It seemed inappropriate.

For a pre-teen boy trying to negotiate his own space and identity within a compact family structure, it was one of the most uncomfortable scenes in cinematic history.

I dedicated myself as an adolescent to assuring that we wouldn't get too physically close. For a couple years, I wouldn't even sit across from her at restaurant tables. Needless to say, there was never, ever any soda flicking.

Okay, you can call your psychiatrist friend now to analyze all the rich Oedipal context from that story. Let me know when you have it all figured out.

But in the meantime, I was *not* going to pluck my mother's chin. No way. A mother and son need distance—even if the mother's in the final phase of her life in a nursing home.

"I can do it," Angel offered, just as simply as if someone had asked him to run an errand to the post office. I was shocked and beyond appreciative.

Angel's broad smile reflected a naturally well-balanced, jovial personality. His shaved head and cinnamon skin might have conjured comparisons with a more compact version of Vin Diesel, but his personality and wardrobe were decidedly brighter. Stick me into any slightly stressful situation and I could spend hours or days overanalyzing and overdramatizing. Angel's feathers weren't easily ruffled, so he balanced me.

Angel often used a Puerto Rican adage to describe my tendency to overcomplicate situations: "buscando las cuatro patas." Literally, it means "looking for four paws" on a cat. In other words, if you search for trouble, you'll find it. You know the cat has four paws. So why waste your time obsessing about it? When I searched the phrase online, the closest I found was "buscarle tres pies al gato sabiendo que tiene cuatro," which means "looking for three paws on a cat when you know it has four." It's a slightly different message, meaning that you shouldn't create unnecessary problems by trying to prove something that's not true. Perhaps Angel's version is a Puerto Rican derivation of that original saying from Spain. At any rate, his no-nonsense approach was something that I admired and tried to emulate.

"If I can find some tweezers in your room, I'll do it right now," he told my mother.

"I'd love that, honey," she nodded, handing Angel a bowl of sour-cream-and-onion dip that he'd made to accompany the shiny bag of potato chips. He set it down and darted into her room, returning a couple minutes later with the requisite instrument in hand.

"I used to watch my mother pluck her chin all the time," he said upon returning, taking a seat in a wingback chair next to my mother's wheelchair. "It's easy."

Without a word, my mother jutted her chin forward as Angel expertly—and apparently painlessly—liberated several gray hairs.

"Thank you, honey," she said, passing her fingers along her now-smooth skin with a satisfied smile. "That feels so much better now."

...

If I had been able to overcome my intimacy issues at an earlier age, my younger self might have welcomed the chance to not only pluck my mother's chin but to give her a total beauty makeover. She had, as long as I could remember, been rather utilitarian when it came to style and fashion—so much so that when I was growing up, I went through a period where I fantasized about creating a luxuriously upgraded Eunice Chesnut.

It was a rather specific image. I pictured her strutting through the heavily fragranced perfume aisles at Sibley's, one of the most upscale department stores in downtown Rochester, impeccably garbed in a gray suit with a neat jacket and knee-length skirt that fit her ample form in the most flattering way. The suit, actually, wasn't that different from one that she already owned, but my imagination accessorized it to the hilt, with gray sling-back pumps, a pair of elegant leather gloves, and a matching purse. The most important effect was the hat: a jaunty felt affair that was a cross between a fedora and something that a female version of Robin Hood might wear, with an overly long gray feather gently flowing back as she strolled, chin up, past the store's most elegantly illuminated display cases. And I'd be walking beside her, the proud son with the cool mother en route to the glamorous restaurant on the store's top floor, where marble columns and giant chandeliers provided the perfect backdrop for elite shoppers to nibble on perfectly sliced club sandwiches as relaxing easy listening music filled the air.

There'd surely be complimentary whisperings about her outfit in the sumptuous ladies' lounge, an upscale restroom on the building's top floor.

The reality was quite different. She did take me to that restaurant a couple times (and I did have the privilege of seeing the ladies' lounge when I was much younger, back when she didn't want me to go to the men's room alone). But when we dined there, she wore something more along the lines of a colorful, polyester Maude-style pantsuit, with a basic blouse and long vest that hid some of her girth.

At Venerable Hills, fashion decisions were left to people I barely knew. A nurse's aide dressed her every morning, choosing from a closet full of apparel she'd bought during her previous life in western New York. With these new chin-plucking requests as well as her need for a haircut, I could finally play a role in some issues related to her vanity, but there'd be no Robin Hood hat.

• • •

Okay, so maybe I *could* do this. If Angel was gutsy enough to pull the hair from his mother-in-law's chin, and they both survived, then I guessed I'd better step up and prove that I was a grown-up too. There was a beauty salon next to the nursing home's lobby, sure, but I saw no point in spending my mother's rapidly evaporating savings on services that I could provide for her.

Back in my apartment, I assembled the tools necessary for a nursing home makeover: tweezers, nail clippers, a pair of scissors, a comb, and a brush. I also bought a bottle of dry shampoo spray, since residents at the nursing home only got one full bath a week, in a tiled room next to the sunroom. I couldn't imagine how it must feel to go that long without a bath or shower. My mother could certainly benefit from having her hair washed more often.

I searched through my collection of airline amenity kits to store the beauty supplies but found something more appropriate: a vintage blue moneybag from the Kentucky bank where my grandparents used to keep their savings, and which also happened to be the long-time workplace of my great uncle Mark, the guy who first introduced my parents to each other in the late 1940s, when my mother was a teenager.

"How would you feel about me giving you a quick haircut?" I asked her the next day, dangling the moneybag in front of her as if I'd just robbed a bank.

"I'd really like that. My hair's getting too long on my forehead and it's starting to cover my eyes."

"Well then, Miss Eunice, let's step right into the Eunice Clayton Chesnut Beauty Salon and fix that," I chirped, rolling her into the bathroom. I grabbed my cell phone and searched for 1940s big-band music before setting it on the ledge. Soon, the lively sounds of the Andrews Sisters echoed off the septic yellow tiles.

My mother tapped her good hand on the arm of the chair as I snipped at her hair and clipped her fingernails. I sprayed the dry shampoo and combed it through her newly neatened locks. My mother touched the side of her head.

"I don't know if I like that spray," she said. "What is it? It just makes my hair feel greasy."

"Sorry about that, Momma," I said. "We can just wait a couple days for them to wash your hair." I finished combing her hair, observing how the brown and gray waves fell into place, not much different from when we went to Sibley's, just grayer.

The irresistible beat of "Boogie Woogie Bugle Boy" filled the air as I noticed a tiny hair standing out from her right jawline. Angel must have missed that one. I smiled as I leaned over with the tweezers, ready to pluck.

18. Confessions of a Pre-Teen Airline Addict

"No sir, you CANNOT have more peanuts!" the red-faced flight attendant shrieked, stabbing a furious finger into the air. "And no, I AM NOT going to give you a goddamned amenity kit. Sit DOWN sir, or I will call the pilot immediately!"

Surprisingly, the trouble-making passenger didn't say a word in response. Actually, it wasn't surprising at all, since there was no passenger. And there was no flight attendant either, for that matter. The irate voice and aggressive finger belonged to a twelve-year-old redheaded boy named J.J. He and I were immersed in a lively game we called "playing stewardess." But our aircraft wasn't a plane at all. It was a rusty, abandoned school bus that sat rotting in a field near my house. J.J. was always the bitchier crewmember during this game, screaming at invisible frequent flyers who had the nerve to complain about the vines growing through the windows or the rusty coils bursting through what remained of the scratchy seats. This was a first-class cabin, dammit, and the flight attendants deserved respect.

J.J. was my best friend in seventh grade and the first kid I'd met who obsessed about travel and airlines as much as I did. Our first encounter took place over the formaldehyde stench of dissected frogs in science class, thanks to a fortuitous alphabetical seating arrangement. People said we looked alike because we both had red hair, but we really didn't. J.J.'s larger frame and more traditional redhead features (blue eyes, light eyebrows) didn't match my slight build and higher-contrast dark eyebrows and eyes. What we did have in common, however, was a passion for air travel.

Most people didn't understand our obsession. Lots of people love to travel, after all. But most people only like the being there, not the getting there. They hate the airline industry, considering it a necessary evil designed to simultaneously transport you to your destination while torturing you with high fares, crowded planes, bad service, and lingering feelings of inadequacy because you never joined the mile high club.

To better understand the mindset that brought J.J. and me together, allow me to take you on a flight into the mind of a seventh-grade misfit wandering the high-ceilinged halls of a middle school set within a beautiful piece of English Tudor revival architecture. I didn't have a lot of friends. Some kids made fun of me. But my once-yearly plane trips to visit my grandparents in Kentucky exposed me to a magical world, a parallel universe where pilots smiled at me and flight attendants doled out free food on trays decorated with sleek airline logos. Flight crews represented the ultimate in globetrotting sophistication, far outweighing the social standing of even the coolest kid or meanest bully in school. Oh sure, those kids wielded some power in the hallowed halls of our beautiful school. But they'd be lost and powerless in the glamorous concourses of Pittsburgh International Airport or Chicago's O'Hare, where only I knew exactly how to get to the Ozark Air Lines gates.

Finding another person who, like me, worshipped the vibrant visuals and exotic glamour of the airline industry gave me a new sense of belonging—although I first discovered our shared passion because J.J. was a great liar. He claimed his father owned an airline.

"What, you've never heard of Catalines International?" he asked. "My father's the president. It's based at the Rochester Airport."

I was a gullible kid so I believed him (I'd spent more of my childhood socializing with my mother's adult friends than with kids my own age, so I still hadn't grasped that many kids were expert liars—and remember, there was no internet that could be used for easy fact checking).

By the time I figured out the truth, we were already well on our way to becoming good friends, and there was no way I could ever drop the only person in the entire middle school who cared about airlines and air travel. J.J. approached the world of air travel with all the spirit and competitiveness of a sports fan, and that pushed us even further. Our click was so potent, in fact, that it would soon lead us beyond playing flight attendant to deceptive impersonations and activities that, I believe, were downright illegal.

• • •

We explored our obsession in myriad ways. To start, I was irked that J.J. had lied to me. If he could own an imaginary airline, why couldn't I? He might have had the guts to concoct a fake company, but he had no visuals to back it up. I was good at drawing airplanes and logos. So, one day I sat down on my red bedspread and created Chesway Global, a sparkling new international carrier with a far-reaching route map. Gorgeous stripes of bright and dark green flowed from my markers onto sketches of the company's first Boeing 747, running beneath the giant *CG* letters emblazoned on the tail.

J.J. seemed mildly impressed with my creation, and it sparked his competitive nature. We found our fake airlines locked in a brutal struggle for dominance in the imaginary marketplace, as we devised increasingly extravagant promotional gimmicks for our airlines.

First, I introduced disco-dancing flight attendants to stage elaborately choreographed shows on Chesway Global's wide-body aircraft. Then J.J. debuted what he called "Hawaiian Kid Centers" on Catalines International's jumbo jets, which basically consisted of strapping lei-wearing, Honolulu-bound children to a jungle gym in the plane's cargo hold. And—in what should have been an obvious sign that we'd grow up to be gay—J.J. and I both fought over which airline would be allowed to contract the Village People to perform on board.

My imagination would gradually take me far beyond the airline industry. While some kids conjured imaginary friends, I invented imaginary corporations and brands. Chesway Global soon became the flagship carrier in the airline division of my vast conglomerate, the MEC Corporation. Other divisions included the Cheston Motor Car Company, a major car manufacturer, National Inns, a mid-priced hotel chain, and ITV, a television network for which I devised an extensive programming schedule featuring second-rate TV stars who I thought might jump at a chance to have their own show on what, in my mind, was the nation's fourth-biggest network (most people didn't have cable TV back then).

All my corporate creations were realized through drawings, sketches, and promotional copy that I crafted while sitting on the red-and-orange shag rug in my bedroom. My fascination with corporate branding would later come to fruition in a meticulously researched high school term paper, enticingly titled "Methods and Effects of Airline Growth." My English teacher gave me a near-perfect ninety-nine as well as a reality check. "This is an extremely well-researched and well-written paper," she told the class as she held up my report, "even though the subject matter is quite dull."

• • •

The only person who understood my corporate fantasy life was J.J., although he was only interested in the airline aspect of it. Like me, J.J. had a bedroom filled with a growing collection of airline memorabilia—random timetables, brochures, and pilot's wings collected on family trips. Soon, we found ourselves competing to amass the largest cache of ephemera, like two junkies amplifying the urge of the other to get a fix.

Our infrequent family air travel provided only minimal opportunities to sustain our addiction, so we decided to go to the source. We started writing letters to every airline for which we could find a mailing address, asking for memorabilia. Our parents graciously paid for the postage (my mother, probably thrilled that I finally had a best friend, would become something of an accomplice in our quest for more collectibles). Surprisingly, nearly every airline responded, filling our mailboxes with travel posters, postcards, and other glamorously designed material.

The problem came when we eventually reached the end of the airline mailing list. We needed a bigger fix: more timetables, more posters, more brochures. How could we continue to add to our booty?

The answer, we decided, lay in our pre-teen voices. The same talent that allowed us to convincingly play agitated female flight attendants aboard the abandoned school bus just might help us to gain access to a trove of fresh airline material. But this time, rather than walking the aisles of an imaginary aircraft, we'd portray middle-aged female travel agents, calling the airlines to ask for help in decorating our agencies.

Was this deceptive? Yes. Was it a scam? Maybe. But it was just the beginning.

For these duplicitous phone conversations, I aimed for a soft yet professional voice, trying to strike a tone that wasn't too girly or too young. My goal was to be a lady who'd seen it all, but who still knows how to smile and be friendly when talking with fellow industry insiders. Like the mean travel agent in Brockport, who was friendly when she talked to grown-ups but yelled "hands off!" at me when she found out I'd called an airline directly about one of our reservations.

"This is Susan over at MEC Airline Service in Brockport, New York," I said to the unlucky airline agent who answered my call. I nervously twisted the phone cord as I stood in the doorway between the kitchen and living room. My eyes landed on J.J., who sat at the dining room table, stretching his hands across the plastic tablecloth while arguing with an invisible client about a hotel reservation (whether flight attendant or travel agent, J.J.'s role playing always involved yelling at customers). To make the scene as realistic as possible, J.J. occasionally pecked at the keys of my portable typewriter, creating office-inspired sound effects by randomly typing and conversing in a low murmur with customers who apparently made unrealistic demands and needed to be told off. MEC Airline Service was a master at customer relations.

I mustered all the professional urgency that I could for the airline representative on the phone. "Well, you see, um, we're redecorating our office, and I'm calling to see if you could send us some travel posters for our agency. Do you think you could do that?"

Surprisingly, several airlines fell for our ploy. Tubes of airline posters began piling up in my bedroom. My mother, in yet another example of complicit permissiveness, agreed to cede me control of the family room so that I could convert it into the Airline Room, a showplace for my commercial aviation treasures (one of the advantages of being a two-person family in a four-bedroom house is that there's a lot of unused space). Soon, National Airlines covered the gray paneled wall with visions of a colorful, tulip-filled vacation in Amsterdam. A timetable holder provided the latest information for anyone dying to know when the next flight to Albany/Schenectady/Troy might depart. An impressionistic New Orleans travel poster brought fresh color to the adjoining guest bathroom.

But then we reached the end of the phone book listings. We still needed more stuff. What else could we do?

• • •

If impersonating a travel agent on the phone was dishonest, our next scheme was just plain criminal. It started on a lazy Saturday, when J.J. and I were draped across the bed and couch in my bedroom, bored as we stared at the airline travel posters that graced my walls.

"Ask your mom to drive us to the airport," J.J. suggested, like it was a normal thing to do.

"What for?"

"Just to walk around and look at the planes. Maybe we can pick up some stuff."

I guess I shouldn't have been surprised that my open-minded mother agreed to my request. She was the perfect enabler.

It felt weirdly exhilarating to visit the airport when we weren't traveling or picking up anyone. With no luggage and Mom not telling me to hurry up or we'd miss our flight, I was free to just wander with my best friend. My mother removed her thick winter coat, took a seat across from one of the ticket counters, and pulled a book and reading glasses from her giant faux-leather purse. "You boys have fun, but let's not stay more than an hour, okay?" And with that, her legs crossed and her head lowered into a thick tome by some author with three names that I thought sounded funny together.

J.J. and I scurried away, enjoying distant whiffs of jet fuel as we charged down the longer of the airport's two concourses where, on the right side, airline posters touted the beauty of Hawaii and Chicago. On the left, Allegheny Airlines had recently upgraded its departure areas to reflect its name change, complete with sumptuous, red-carpeted walls and glossy posters showcasing the sun-drenched beauty of Tampa/St. Petersburg/Clearwater.

Suddenly, there was a shuffle of airport staff around one gate. We eavesdropped and learned that a technical issue had forced a Syracuse-bound North Central Airlines flight to make an unscheduled landing in Rochester. For young airline nerds, witnessing the unexpected arrival of an airline that didn't normally serve your airport was the equivalent of a zoologist spotting a wild elephant on the Pampas of Argentina. Seeing a flight attendant from the exotic, Minneapolis-based carrier would be almost a religious experience. So when we noticed an elegantly poised woman exiting the jetway wearing a pantsuit in the airline's signature blue and teal tones, we immediately ran over and excitedly accused her of working for the company.

"Excuse me," J.J. blurted. "Aren't you a North Central Airlines stewardess?"

The woman looked at us blankly. "No, I'm not," she said curtly as she walked away.

I'm not sure what we would have said next if she had, in fact, been a member of the flight crew. Apparently, all the flight attendants stayed on board the plane. Disappointed, we watched as more passengers deplaned and later reboarded to complete their trip for Syracuse.

The concourse grew quiet again.

Since it was Saturday, there were few flights and most gates were empty and unstaffed, their check-in counters temptingly laden with timetables and brochures. But we already had most of that stuff. How boring.

"We should just take the whole display rack," J.J. said, pointing at a gate. "No one's around."

Well, it was true. No one would see what we did; there were no security cameras and no one walking around. Before I knew it, I was playing lookout as J.J. swept in and grabbed the entire display box, zipping it inside his oversized winter jacket.

We scurried down the corridor to the next gate.

"Now you do it," J.J. said. "I'll be the lookout."

I was the kind of kid who feared authority. Any kind of run-in could bring the kind of sphincter-tightening reaction that would make me feel like I was about to crap my pants. If I got caught, I'd be in deep shit, possibly literally.

But there was a really cool airline display rack there on that counter, just waiting to find a home in my Airline Room.

"Okay, I'll do it, but just be careful," I warned. "Let me know as soon as you see anyone coming." I darted over to the counter and took the display case. I looked back at J.J., who stood in the middle of the concourse.

"There's no one around," he whispered, waving his hands in a circular motion. "Keep looking!"

I felt like a contestant on a game show where you only get one minute to grab all the dollars you can while locked inside a vertical wind tunnel. I opened drawers and rifled through them, grabbing pads of paper with airline logos. I spun around quickly and nervously eyed the departure board—back then, there were no electronic displays, just plastic numbers and strips with destination names, which agents would slide in and out as needed. I turned toward J.J., who nodded and mouthed the word "yes!" I quickly reached up and slid the destination signs and flight numbers out of their slots and into my coat.

J.J. started waving his hands like a guy trying to stop a bus. Out of the corner of my eye, I saw a man in a suit walking purposefully down the concourse toward us. I had to get out of there, and fast. I darted from behind the counter to my best friend's side, desperately trying to keep the stolen goods from tumbling out from my coat.

J.J. was an expert at creating distractions and immediately took on the role of some bizarre, teenaged frequent flyer, in an effort to show the approaching man that we had every right to be standing in front of an empty gate. "So anyway, as I was telling my friend Gloria, you simply *must* fly first class to Hawaii," he gushed loudly, trying to sound as much like an urban sophisticate as a pale, pre-teen boy in a gigantic winter coat could be. The man cocked his head a bit as he looked our way, but then continued past the gate.

We walked carefully toward the front of the airport, our hands tightly pressed against our coats to prevent any prizes from slipping out, grinning with the satisfaction of completing our first round of a game we'd come to call gate raiding (you might more accurately call it stealing).

Whether my mother was aware of our actions, I'll never know. But she surely must have wondered why my bedroom was suddenly decked out with signs announcing exact departure times for nonstop service to Washington's National Airport. My bedroom—which had recently been painted red—was already as close an approximation to a departure lounge as a twelve-year-old boy could make it. I even took the old living room couch, which my mother was going to throw out, and draped it in red fabric to serve as a waiting area for imaginary passengers.

I realized that J.J. and I might never fully satisfy our voracious hunger for airline memorabilia. But at least I'd found a friend who was as excited about the hunt as I was.

19. My Father's Ghost

New York City, October 2015

A letter appeared in my mailbox on one chilly afternoon in October. It came from a seventy-year-old Dutch man I'd never heard of. He had found my name and address online and decided to contact me to ask questions about a childhood experience that still haunted him. DIn December 1943, when he was six years old,he had witnessed the crash of the Flying Fortress aircraft my father had been co-piloting when the Nazis shot him down.

I devoured the entire letter before going up to my apartment, and then rushed over to the nursing home to show my mother.

"Isn't that amazing, Momma?" I asked, waving the letter excitedly after rolling her into the library. "After all these years, we hear from someone who saw Daddy's plane crash!"

I realized that she may not have fully understood, but my excitement seemed to catch her interest. "Wow, that's really a surprise, sweetie," she said, reaching out her hand as I sat on the couch. "Let me take a look at that."

She took the paper and scanned it like someone would look at a painting. I knew she couldn't interpret the words, so I read a few of the best parts to her, realizing the Dutch man's imperfect English might have made it even more difficult to comprehend.

In the afternoon of the 13th of December 1943, my father and I were at the distribution office in Kloosterburen. My daddy was a leader of the office. A police officer also was there for some investigations. Suddenly, the policeman shouted, "Hey, come on, go, get out of here, a burning airplane comes here right away!" He pointed in the direction of the window.

Yes, indeed, I saw a burning airplane coming down.

We all ran as fast as we could to the road. We jumped over the ditch and ran away through the field.

My father's aircraft crashed in a field outside of town. The entire crew had bailed out with parachutes, and the Nazis captured them.

The whole afternoon, the burning plane was to be seen; a thick black smoke was over Molenry for hours!

I am seventy years old now. I always wanted to find out what exactly happened.

Thanks to online research, the man learned that my father was the copilot of that plane.

I found out that the crew bailed out on time, over a village called Pieterburen, about six miles from Molenry.

The crew was captured and had been transported to the POW camp Stalag Luft 1, Barth-Vogelsang in Germany.

The man said he spoke with a neighbor, who recalled that at age sixteen he had witnessed the aircraft descending without realizing they were in danger. He and a friend leaned their bicycles against the railings along a canal. "Suddenly, we were covered with mud and soil," the man told him, adding that a large piece of metal hit his bike. Thinking the material could be used on his family's houseboat, he took it aboard. "After three days, two German soldiers came and ordered us to hand over the object. Two days later the soldiers came back and gave eighty Dutch Guilders to my daddy for a new bike."

He closed the letter with a request for details about my father's experience. "I hope you have some more information about the crew of the B-17 and of course from your father, for they did such a good job with severe danger of life for our liberty and freedom."

• • •

In previous decades, my mother researched her late husband's World War II experiences, as part of her master's degree in history. Long after my father had died, she interviewed his first pilot about how the crew had lost two engines while under attack, jumped at about nineteen thousand feet just before the right wing came off, and were captured by Nazis soon after reaching the ground.

My father, meanwhile, documented as much of his wartime experiences as permitted, through letters to his family and my mother (who at that point wasn't even his girlfriend yet). "Nothing of great interest has happened here recently," he wrote in his final letter to his mother before the final, ill-fated mission, "and my luck still holds."

Daddy's luck ran out, however on December 13, 1943. A Western Union telegram arrived at his brother Aubrey's home, stating in large type:

YOUR BROTHER SECOND LIEUTENANT JOHN J CHESNUT JR HAS BEEN REPORTED MISSING IN ACTION SINCE THIRTEEN DECEMBER IN EUROPEAN AREA PERIOD.

They didn't find out until early 1944 that he was a prisoner of war. My mother saved nearly all his subsequent letters, some of which documented the beginning of their romantic relationship.

My parents didn't have a traditional courtship. They'd met through my mother's uncle Mark, who was living with her family in Louisville in the 1930s. "John would come home with Mark sometimes for dinner," my mother told me decades later, describing my father as tall, handsome, and dark-haired. "And then he enlisted in World War II. While he was in Texas training to be a pilot, he started writing me letters, and I wrote back to him. I never really had a date with him. He was almost nine years older than me. I was seventeen. It was really just a correspondence romance. And then he was gone so long, I didn't see him again until after the war."

My father continued to write to my mother from the prisoner-of-war camp at Stalag Luft I, on Germany's Baltic coast. After his release in 1945, he returned to Kentucky and immediately started talking about marriage, mailing my mother an insistent message from his parents' Baileys Switch home to my mother in Louisville.

I love you Eunice, and I'm having great difficulty being patient while all my old friends cross-question me. I want to be with you. Do you really love me Eunice? Perhaps I overemphasize it, but were you really reluctant to make certain concessions to our partnership? I told you as best I could what I think and what I plan to do. When I come back next week we will be able to make the important decisions.

• • •

I'm not sure if the reference to "concessions" was about sex or marriage, but at any rate, my mother wasn't crazy about the idea of tying the knot with someone she'd never really dated.

"He said that he wanted to get married right then, and I said, 'No, I don't want to do that yet,'" she recalled. "He said, 'Well then I'm leaving.' So I said, 'Well, then okay, let's get married.'"

Such was life in the 1940s. A good Southern Baptist girl didn't turn down a marriage proposal from a decent man.

My mother later credited her wartime correspondence with attracting her future husband. "I was a good letter writer," she told me. "That's why he married me. But after the wedding, he found out I could write better than I could keep house."

My parents got married on a humid, sunny day in August of 1945 at the West Broadway Baptist Church, my mother's place of worship in Louisville's middle-class West End neighborhood. John wore his Army Air Force uniform and Eunice donned a light blue suit and a feathered hat that looked like a dead bird was nesting on her head—a sartorial statement that would be a source of great amusement for the two children she'd later have.

. . .

Now, my mother sat in a shiny wheelchair in a spotlessly clean nursing home, more than forty years after her husband's death, holding a letter from a man who saw his plane crash more than half a century earlier.

"Isn't that cool that he found me and decided to send a letter?" I asked.

"That really is interesting," my mother answered. "So he was writing to you about your father?"

20. Feeling Insecure? An Airline Makeover Might Be Just What You Need

Are you a teenage boy who doesn't quite fit in? Self-conscious about your stringy red hair, pale skin, girlish walk, and lackluster reputation at school? Intimidated by the popular kids, the jocks, the bullies, and even the brains? Maybe your ego could use a jet-powered jumpstart infused with airline-inspired glamour.

Okay, so maybe that's not you; it was me a few decades ago. And maybe today, at a time when passengers complain about overcrowded planes and canceled flights, the airline industry is the last place you'd look for inspiration about anything. And yes, most teenage boys look to sports, music, academics, or even religion for their role models. But I wasn't most teenage boys.

Back when I was an insecure kid, I bolstered my self-esteem by studying the time-tested marketing and branding strategies of some of the nation's most trend-setting airlines. Follow these helpful tips and you just might find your self-confidence rising faster than a table tray returning to its fully upright and locked position.

Go for a bold new look. We have advertising guru Mary Wells Lawrence to thank for turning a once-dowdy, Dallas-based airline into the hippest midcentury way to fly. Her "End of the Plain Plane" campaign, which debuted in the late 1960s, showcased a vibrant, head-to-toe transformation that included "space bubble" flight attendant helmets by Italian fashion guru Emilio Pucci and cheerily pastel-colored planes revamped by celebrity designer Alexander Girard (back then, nearly all commercial aircraft were either boring white or unimaginative silver). Braniff's "Air Strip" advertisements, meanwhile, emphasized the brand's sex appeal by showing flight attendants seductively removing various multicolored layers of their Pucci uniforms. It doesn't matter that those days are long gone, the lesson still applies.

The lesson: Change your style to fit the times. Why not treat yourself to some multicolored corduroy pants and patch-work jeans? You'll convert those drab middle school hallways into a runway for the jet-set!

Don't worry if people don't understand. In the middle of the twentieth century, a famed billionaire businessman named Howard Hughes owned TWA, one of the nation's most glamorous international airlines. Movie stars posed for publicity photos as they boarded his planes. But after he sold that carrier, he decided to take on a more interesting challenge. In 1968, he bought a much smaller regional airline called Air West. To give the company flair, he renamed it Hughes Airwest, slathered the planes in fresh canary-colored paint, outfitted the flight attendants in eye-catching Sundance Yellow dresses and dramatic capes trimmed in Universe Blue. To drive home the airline's new, cutting-edge image, he commissioned a magnificently mod, nearly illegible font to flaunt the new name.

All this glorious fuss for a strictly regional airline that served obscure Western cities like Redding/Red Bluff, Pullman/Moscow, and Pasco/Kennewick/Richland. It didn't matter if most people hadn't heard of those destinations or could barely read the trend-setting signage in the off-beat font. The billionaire had no interest in trying to make his airline blend in. He stressed uniqueness.

The lesson: You don't have to be the biggest or the best to stand out. Don't be afraid to be different. When your eighth-grade teacher tells the class to make name labels for the upcoming Washington trip, use the airline's font as inspiration, so your name is nearly indecipherable—but totally cool.

Change your flight plan. In the old days, people showed their dislike of some airlines by making up rude nicknames for them. Some people called Pittsburgh-based Allegheny Airlines "Agony Airlines," for example. But the scrappy little carrier fought back, repainting its planes with confident, thick red stripes and extending its route map beyond its former boundaries to reach far-off lands in Florida and Arizona. Then came the big news: the airline would be reborn as USAir. It was like an aspiring actor moving to Hollywood and taking on a new identity for maximum celebrity effect.

The lesson: Reimagine yourself and how you present yourself to the public. And most importantly: believe the advertising and the positive messages that you create, even if it's just in your head.

Observing the dazzling visuals and clever marketing ploys of these forward-thinking airlines, I learned that you could be small, you could be different, you could even weather insults. You didn't need to be like everyone else. You just needed the right positioning in the marketplace. I studied enough magazine ads, timetables, and TV commercials to realize that the biggest, most popular airlines weren't the most interesting or the most inventive. Underdogs can be cool.

The same is true today. Think about which airline advertising catches your eye the most. I bet it's not one of the biggest carriers.

I didn't have to be friends with the most popular people at school. Kids could still make fun of me for sucking at sports. Some of them might call me names. But it was up to me to build my own brand. And I could make it whatever I wanted.

If a billionaire could recast a tiny airline as one of the most fabulous and colorful creations in the sky, I should be able to reposition myself and find a place in the world too.

21. Salvation vs. Star Wars

Benton, 1977

The lyrics of the gospel song "Where He Leads Me I Will Follow," written by Salvation Army officer Ernest W. Blandy, dated back to 1890, but the pull was very much in the present as we sang them on one steamy Sunday morning in western Kentucky. In between verses, the pink-faced preacher—who all the grown-ups called Brother Eustace—raised his hand from the blond wood pulpit and the singing would stop, even as the organ kept playing.

"Isn't it time that you accepted Jesus Christ as your personal Lord and Savior?" he asked, scanning the room with wide eyes. "Or perhaps you accepted him a very long time ago, but you have let your faith lapse. *Now* is the time to come back."

I looked around at the sea of people, clad in the candy colors of summer. Some cooled themselves with promotional fans from the nearby funeral home. A woman wearing a brightly patterned blouse and a man wearing a pastel tie started to cry, their faces bunching up and their eyes squinting. My mother and grandfather stood silently on either side of me, waiting for an indication to sing the next line.

I had witnessed this call to salvation many times at the Southern Baptist church that my grandparents attended. And every week during every visit, my grandfather (who we

145

all called Pop) and I would go to our respective, age-appropriate Sunday school classes; he'd carry a well-worn Bible and big yellow notepad with his lesson plan for the older men's class that he taught. For some reason my mother didn't go to Sunday school, even though there was one for grown-up ladies. But she'd usually join us for the church service. My grandmother was always kind of sickly—something about her heart being too big or something—so she stayed home and watched a bunch of ministers on TV.

The organ music rose again, and we all started singing.

The crying woman gently pushed her husband aside, one hand to her face as she walked toward the front of the sanctuary, sobbing. The minister smiled and spread his arms wide, like one of those guys at the airport who tells the planes where to park. Well, that lady sure did understand runway language because she picked up the pace of her steps and went right to him, giving him a hug before stepping back and facing the audience, her eyes overflowing and her body shaking.

"We welcome you back, sister Lena," Brother Eustace said. "Now, who else would like to come and renew themselves in front of our Lord and be born again?"

My mind started churning.

Am I supposed to be doing that too? Should I go up there?

I knew the preacher would be leading us through this routine for at least fifteen or twenty minutes like he always did at least once a month. This wasn't going to end soon.

The music, the emotion, the tears, the repeated verses urging us to follow. It was hypnotizing, like a tractor beam. Or a timeshare sales talk.

It makes sense, doesn't it? We should all confess our sins and be reborn so we can be good people and go on with our lives.

No one in my family had ever gone up to the front of the church. We'd all been baptized, of course, like you're supposed to do when you're around age twelve. My main motivation for participating in that act of salvation, however, was that it gave me a chance to stand in a big pool of water in the front of my church up North. How often do you get to stand in a mini swimming pool in church?

About two years had passed since my baptism. Did I need to renew myself at age fourteen? No family member ever talked about being saved *again*; that was a topic usually addressed by preachers in church or on TV—like when my grandmother watched the televangelists who praised missionaries for supposedly saving people in Africa and Asia. But not even Gran had ever told me to run up to the front of the church bawling my eyes out. My mother never talked about religion at all, even though we went to church every single Sunday, whether we were in New York or Kentucky.

Still, the music was pulling me. And the preacher kept talking.

I really need to do this. I need to start my life over, from scratch. Things will be better then. I will know what to do with my life and everything will be better.

My mother stood between me and the aisle. I'd have to push past her and then walk all the way up to the stage. And everyone would be looking at me.

What if I go up but I don't cry? Will people think I'm weird if I'm not crying? And what am I supposed to say to people after I accept the Lord again? Is it like a job interview? I don't know what I'm supposed to say. I didn't really feel like I accepted any Lord after my real baptism. I honestly didn't feel any different. So what's this supposed to feel like now?

"Sister Lena, do you accept Jesus Christ as your personal Lord and Savior?" the minister asked.

"I do, I do." Lena nodded, her face so wet and red it looked like she'd just gone swimming on a really sunny day.

"There is room for more," he said, turning to the audience. The organ swelled, and we sang another line.

I really need to do this.

I bunched up the green polyester of my leisure suit pants with one hand and wrapped the other around the hymnal. My

mother's soft singing rang in my left ear, and Pop's enthusi-
astically loud voice—which sometimes sounded more like
yelling than singing—vibrated from the right.

*But maybe I can wait until I get back to Brockport. They
don't do these calls to salvation at the Baptist Church there,
so I can just talk to Mr. Warner and make a special request.
He wouldn't make a dramatic scene or embarrass me in front
of everyone. Mr. Warner never pushes religion on people, especially if he knows they don't feel comfortable.*

This contrast between my two ministers was understand-
able since they represented two different types of Baptist
church. In the South, our church was a member of the
Southern Baptist Convention, the largest Protestant denom-
ination in the United States and the world's biggest Baptist
group. Its congregations split off from Northern Baptists in
1845, and its evangelical approach meant that parishioners
talked a lot about being saved. The American Baptist Association, meanwhile, was founded in 1924 as an association of
independent churches over which the main organization has
no direct control. Our Northern church didn't stage monthly
public salvations and our minister didn't talk about religion
in personal conversations unless you really wanted to.

In the South, we called the minister "Reverend so-and-so" or
"Brother so-and-so." In the North, it was just "Mr. Warner."

*I can just make an appointment to be saved privately with
Mr. Warner. Yes, that's what I'll do. I don't need to go up
front now.*

I stayed put next to my mother and grandfather until the
last person was reborn, and then rode home in Pop's gigantic,
maroon sedan to pick up Gran and head out for chicken and
dumplings at the Iron Kettle.

For the next couple of weeks, my usual Kentucky diver-
sions distracted me from thoughts of salvation. I stayed busy
visiting various great uncles and aunts, spotting wild bison at
the wildlife preserve at Land Between the Lakes, and riding
bikes with my Kentucky best friend (I had dual lives as a

child, with one best friend in New York and one in Kentucky, one bicycle in New York and one in Kentucky).

I didn't need to feel secure with the Lord for now because I felt safe anyway in the little town of Benton. Even on nights when I stayed out after dark with my friend at the gas station where he worked after school, there was a grown-up who protected me: a towering, mentally challenged man I knew only as Bird Dog.

"Y'all have a big time?" Bird Dog would ask every single night as he walked me through the darkened streets to Pop and Gran's house, his immense arm draped over my skinny shoulder. I knew I should have been too old to be scared, but Bird Dog seemed to recognize that I didn't like to walk alone at night, and with him I felt like nothing bad would ever happen.

Even going back to church—albeit a different one—didn't reawaken my curiosity about being saved. The following Sunday, we went to a church farther out in the country, the preferred place of worship for much of our extended family of great uncles, great aunts, and cousins. The congregation there favored bouncier, country gospel music, with lots of hand-clapping and harmonizing. It was harder to get bored during their services, and the warm welcome from all those family members who I barely knew made me feel special. And there was no call for salvation on the Sunday we visited, so I didn't have to worry about a religious tractor beam pulling me in.

At my grandparents' house, I continued to volunteer to recite the traditional prayer before meals.

Our Father in heaven, accept our thanks for this food, forgive our sins, we ask in Jesus's name, amen.

Pop liked it when I said the prayer, and I liked to please him. I also liked talking in front of an audience.

As the summer weeks wound down, it was time to start loading my mother's car for the two-day trip back to Brockport. I'd have plenty of time to think about everything. We hugged my grandparents and pulled out of their circular driveway, watching them wave from the family room window.

"What do you think about those people who go up to the front of the church to get reborn?" I asked as I watched Benton disappear in the rear window.

"I think it's wonderful that people find comfort in their religion," she said as she steered the giant car onto the western Kentucky Parkway toward Louisville. "For some people, that's all they have, and it's what gets them through hard times. Sometimes I wish I could have faith like that."

"But do you think that people really get saved?"

"I think the church provides help and support to a lot of people in need. The church can do a lot of good work."

"But what about heaven and hell and being saved and all that stuff?"

"I don't think all of those details are necessarily true."

"What about the stuff in the Bible?"

"The Bible is an important book. It provides comfort to people who need it. But I don't know that it's one hundred percent based on facts."

• • •

Back in Brockport, I fell into my Sunday morning tradition of sitting on a hard wooden pew at the Baptist Church, bored out of my wits. My eyes scanned the sanctuary for anything that might be more interesting than the sermon: the older woman sitting near us whose outdated clothing made her look like a witch, the travel agent lady in the choir with long blonde hair who I wished would share the secrets of the airline industry with me, the colorful stained-glass windows that were framed by what appeared like otherworldly, faceless humans with outstretched arms.

Sometimes I'd pretend I had to go to the bathroom during church service and wander the building, exploring a parlor I called God's Living Room because it was furnished with couches and comfy chairs where I imagined God and Jesus might hang out, reading magazines and entertaining visitors.

After every service, Mr. Warner would always engage me in a polite conversation about school or pop culture. He knew I was interested in the airline industry, so he would bring that up sometimes. He even knew about *Star Wars* and impressed me with his knowledge of R2-D2 and C-3PO.

I never asked him for that appointment to be saved. I guess I knew I wouldn't, even when I was feeling the pull at the church in Kentucky.

• • •

The next summer, Mr. Warner and his wife (who also happened to be my Sunday school teacher) took their annual month-long vacation. Laypeople took over his duties while he was gone. And for some reason, my mother signed us up to lead an entire Sunday service—the whole hour, from start to finish. She wanted me to write and present the main sermon. She may not have believed everything in the Bible, but she respected what the church did for some people and she liked the members of our church. She also liked to be in front of an audience even more than I did. We did go to church every Sunday, anyway, so I guess we were as qualified as anyone.

I loved the idea of performing, but I was too lazy and uninspired to actually sit down and write a sermon. I didn't have a clue what I should say to the congregation.

Finally, when the service was only three days away, my mother started losing patience.

"Do I have to write this god-damned sermon for you?" she asked.

It was almost the same as when I was supposed to mow the lawn and didn't. As usual, I'd put off a chore, she yelled, and then she ended up doing the work herself. She titled the sermon "All I Have Seen" and placed all the words in my mouth, about how, despite my youth, I had already witnessed the bountiful goodness of people's hearts and good deeds, or something like that.

My mother's words and my presentation were sufficiently impressive that, when Mr. Warner heard about it, he sent me a congratulatory note that said he'd be very pleased to write me a letter of recommendation to study at a divinity school if I felt the calling.

I thanked Mr. Warner the next time I saw him in person but ignored his suggestion. And he never bothered me about it. He just kept being the cool kind of minister who was ready to talk about *Star Wars* if I wanted to.

22. The Flight of the Blue Heron

Louisville, 1930s-1960s

The blue heron should know more about my family than I do. Of course, the blue heron really doesn't know anything. It's just a piece of sculpture. But it's been around for more pivotal moments in my family's history than any human, so sometimes I wish it did. Because our own memories are fading.

I imagine how the elegant curve of the heron's torso first caught the eye of my grandmother, Eunice Earle New Clayton, when she saw it in one of Louisville's swanky downtown department stores. Perched gracefully in a sculpted dish designed to hold flowers, the bird was more contemporary than most pottery, a fourteen-inch-tall creation bathed in a muted shade of delphinium blue that seemed to change tone depending on the light. Its Streamline Moderne form, which resembled Art Deco but with fewer distracting details, rendered the bird so aerodynamic that it looked ready to shoot through the air like an elegant bullet.

That surely would look nice on the dining room table, Eunice must have thought. A sturdy woman with a broad nose and square face, she was drawn to pretty things. Her carefully curated outfits—gloves, dress, heels, and hat—attested to her sense of style and desire to follow the cues of the educated Southern middle class of the 1930s. She liked to decorate her home with items that might generate conversation with her neighbors. Eunice never mentioned it, as far as I know, but her quest for beauty may have been a decades-old reaction to the psychological unpleasantness she'd experienced as a child, when her father—who was a teenager when she was born—called her "ugly," "stupid," and "pig" and banished her to live in a boarding house run by her grandparents in Dawson Springs, a western Kentucky town known in the early twentieth century for its therapeutic spas and mineral baths.

As Eunice admired the heron, I imagine that a smiling salesclerk, eager to make a sale, would have informed her that she wasn't looking at just any old bird. This was a genuine piece of Bauer Pottery, a legendary studio with California glamour and Kentucky roots. Was it a coincidence that the creations of a company founded in Paducah attracted my grandmother, not far from her western Kentucky birthplace? Did the salesperson tout the brand's local roots, or focus solely on its Golden State allure? I'll never know. But I do know that after founder John A. Bauer moved his company to Los Angeles in 1909, its colorful ceramic tableware and home décor gained a devoted nationwide following. Even Hollywood showed some love when Joan Crawford's character stocked her kitchen with Bauer mixing bowls in the Oscar-winning movie *Mildred Pierce*.

Pondering whether to make the purchase, Eunice probably turned to her husband, my grandfather, Charles Dexter Clayton. A permissive and doting man with a receding hairline and round spectacles that made him look older than he really was, he would have agreed wholeheartedly that yes, the piece would look just fine in their home, and yes, their neighbor Mrs. Weiss would probably think it was the most beautiful thing too. Soon after, the carefully boxed heron joined Eunice and Charles aboard a rumbling streetcar headed to the West End, a leafy, middle-class neighborhood where the Claytons lived in one of the countless small brick homes.

The blue heron alighted atop the thick wooden dining table, where Eunice often embellished the sculpture with a delicate flourish of sweet pea flowers. She appreciated the multi-sensory beauty of their tissue-thin red petals and light fragrance. Nearly every evening at suppertime, Eunice moved the bird to the credenza to make room for the meal—steaming bowls of Southern staples like beef stew overflowing with potatoes, heaping side dishes of collard greens and okra, and giant plates of crispy fried chicken, which Eunice described as "greezy" rather than "greasy."

The bird maintained its silent perch as three children grew up in that Louisville household. Being a piece of inanimate pottery, it couldn't hear Rarene, the oldest yet most petite child, nimbly teasing big band melodies from the keys of the family's cabinet grand piano, as Don, the youngest child and only boy, belted out the lyrics. It didn't notice as the middle child, my mother—who was confusingly named Eunice, after her own mother—progressed from paper dolls and roller skates to street softball and writing plays for neighborhood kids to perform. If the heron had been sentient, it might have smiled when the younger Eunice returned from watching ten-cent gangster movie matinees at the Shawnee Theatre, daydreaming about being the gun moll of George Raft, a rakishly handsome actor known for his rat-a-tat-tat gangster roles in the 1930s and 1940s.

The blue heron didn't notice that Charles, who everyone called Pop, was absent for several days every month, roaming the far corners of the Bluegrass State as a railway mail clerk for the United States Post Office Department. His career with the predecessor of the US Postal Service provided stable work that carried the family comfortably through the Great Depression. He and his wife had made a wise decision to move to Louisville years earlier, leaving their previous jobs as one-room schoolhouse teachers—roles they accepted before they'd even graduated from college in rural western Kentucky.

The blue heron was equally unresponsive when a tall, dark-haired man named John Jacob Chesnut, Jr.—a coworker of Pop's brother—paid a suppertime visit on one humid evening. Neither the bird nor the younger Eunice could have guessed that the handsome young man would eventually become her husband. Despite her movie-fueled fantasies, my mother's destiny didn't involve being a gangster's girlfriend.

Brockport, 1960s-2010s

When Charles and Eunice Clayton retired back to Kentucky's western reaches in the early 1960s, they sent the blue heron on a different path, migrating north to land on a clean white shelf in John and Eunice Chesnut's brand-new house in western New York State. They'd married right after John returned from his World War II service and moved to Atlanta and then Ann Arbor for him to study at Emory University and the University of Michigan, respectively. He'd halted his PhD program in Ann Arbor to accept a position teaching English in Brockport, a picturesque village on the Erie Canal in western New York. After years of saving, they built a roomy split-level home that was perfect for their growing family; with clapboard siding the color of crusted blood (it looked prettier than it sounds), a soaring cathedral ceiling, and a doorbell that chimed with all the middle-class confidence of a TV commercial.

For the younger Eunice, the ceramic bird was a welcome addition to her new living space, a souvenir of her happy childhood and a symbol of the continuity of the generations. The heron's graceful, Streamline Moderne curves provided a striking contrast to the angular mid-century lines of the vaulted ceiling and fuzzy wall-to-wall carpeting that smothered the living and dining room floor.

The bird remained ageless. It stayed slim even as Eunice became plump during her pregnancy with me and passed no judgment when she never quite regained her original figure.

The sculpted lines of its feathers remained perfectly coiffed even as my mother's loose brown curls fell out of place when she went too long between haircuts. Unlike my grandmother, the younger Eunice was less concerned with aesthetics and more with words and ideas, perhaps because she didn't need to compensate for a difficult childhood like her mother had.

The heron's soothing blue tone never faded from the smoke of my father's frequent cigarettes. It never absorbed the odors of the beef goulash or other exotic dishes that my mother had learned to prepare for dinner guests. Several of those invited friends admired the blue heron and—noticing the empty shelves around it—began bringing Eunice decorative items as gifts, leading to the creation of what she called the blue glass collection, even though the objects were made from a variety of materials. The ever-growing display was decidedly off-limits to me, their young son, and was of no interest whatsoever to Glynn, my teenage sister.

John died of lung cancer at age fifty-one. My forty-three-year-old mother decided the house was too big, especially since Glynn was departing for college and there would be only two of us left. My mother found tenants to occupy the house, and she and I moved to an apartment just in time for me to start kindergarten. The blue heron went into storage. After a year or so, Mom found the smaller digs too confining, so we returned to the big red house, and so did the bird. Its monochromatic blue eyes stared blankly as my mother went back to school and got her undergraduate and graduate degrees. They didn't blink when I headed off to college or when the front door opened to welcome Eunice's two new housemates: her older sister Rarene (who, with Eunice's help, had just left her husband) and Pop (who arrived when my grandmother—the woman who'd first found the bird—passed away). A few years later, Pop died and Rarene moved to live near her son. My mother lived alone in the house for the first time. The heron stayed on.

New York City, 2010s

The blue heron flew, albeit wrapped in newspaper aboard a regional jet, to my apartment in New York City. Many years had passed, and Glynn and I had convinced my mother to move to a more manageable apartment in a fifty-five-and-over complex. My mother gave away most of her furnishings as she prepared to sell the house, and my sister had no interest in any of it. Like my grandmother, I appreciated the sculpture's beauty, and like my mother, I valued its sentimental symbolism. And like many gay men, I gravitated toward mid-century décor.

In a few years, maybe, I could pass the blue heron on to my niece, Emelyne, accompanied by all the stories that happened in its presence. If not, well, Bauer's early creations had appreciated in value. I could always hock it.

"You're bringing too much stuff home from your mother's house," my husband Angel complained when I told him about my plans to adopt the heron. But being a patient man and recognizing our lack of significant décor, he gave in and allowed the bird—as well as a few other choice pieces from the blue glass collection—to land in our apartment. We had a perfect place for the heron: a recessed, built-in shelf in the dining room. It was an original feature dating to the building's 1939 construction—right around the peak of Bauer Pottery's initial fame.

The blue heron was exposed to a variety of new elements in New York City: music by Madonna. The aroma of marijuana. People speaking Spanish. For the first time, it stood in the background during parties marked by the clinking of gold-leafed champagne glasses that someone had given my parents as a wedding gift.

My mother arrived in New York City three years later to check into a nursing home. She was smaller, thinner, her thinking muddled by a brain tumor and maybe Alzheimer's disease.

"Where am I?" she kept asking from her wheelchair in the antiseptic sunroom as we sipped cola from gleaming red cans and munched potato chips from a bright green bag. One day, Angel responded by flashing his vibrant and comforting smile and grabbing a well-worn notebook from her nightstand. He sketched a map of the neighborhood, drawing a star to indicate the location of the nursing home where she lived and another to show our apartment building. She scanned it appreciatively, but the following day repeated the same question.

I had an idea. Maybe visiting Angel's and my apartment—and seeing a few things from her past—would bring some clarity, spark some memories. Especially the blue heron. It was the largest item that had been passed down through the three generations, and my mother had always told me about how it had graced the dining room table when she was growing up. Perhaps the bird could help her to connect the past to the present.

The next day I rolled her away from the nursing home's fluorescent glow, carefully navigating the city's notoriously uneven sidewalks to reach the service entrance of our six-story brick building.

"You see that, Momma?" I asked as we entered the apartment, pointing at the sculpture on my dining room shelf. "That's the blue heron! Your mother used to put flowers around it on the dining room table in your house—1004 South 40th Street in Louisville. Then you had it in your house in Brockport until you let me steal it from you. Remember that?"

She gazed up at the figure.

"Oh yes, I see it," she said slowly, pointing a wrinkled finger. "That's very nice you have that." She frowned and looked around the room. "But do I *live* here?"

The quick change of subject made it clear that she didn't recognize the bird. More pressing issues weighed on her mind—namely, trying to figure out where she was. I placed a hand on her shoulder and explained that she lived just a few blocks away, that this apartment was Angel's and my home, and that we were very happy to be so close to her.

I remembered what she'd told me when I first asked her if I could take the blue heron from her home. "Take whatever you want," she said. "Those are just *things*, and I've got too many *things*."

I couldn't bear to ask my mother if she remembered anything else right now. I wheeled her back to the nursing home. It was the last time she saw the blue heron.

23. How Secret Agents Made Me Horny for Ohio

Columbus, 1979

Let's get one thing straight: I'm sure I didn't *really* want to be molested by anonymous traveling businessmen when I was fourteen years old. And—luckily for me—I never was. But that doesn't mean that I didn't try to catch the eye of handsomely besuited road warriors while wandering the lushly carpeted corridors of the Cordial Court Motor Inn near Columbus, Ohio.

I also don't mean to make light of those who've actually experienced molestation, of course. Sexual abuse is serious, and it can scar victims for life. But as a young teen, I didn't fully comprehend the terminology. All I knew was that I had urges. I was attracted to men. And, back in the 1970s, there was no internet to provide me with educational resources. My mother certainly had no idea what was on my mind and couldn't set me straight (in any sense of the word). She was blissfully unaware that my nascent libido went into overdrive during road trips between our home in western New York State and our extended family in Kentucky.

Before we go into the logistics of my lustful adolescent quest in the Buckeye State, let's try to understand why such a bizarre combination of words—"anonymous traveling businessmen" and "molestation"—bounced around my head as I sauntered down the hotel halls. First: the men I saw there were usually dressed in suits, so they were obviously *businessmen*. Second, they were staying at a hotel, so clearly they were *traveling*. And third, I had no idea who they were or where they were from. So they were *anonymous*. And what, pray tell, would you call it if a grown man were to show romantic interest in an affection-starved teenage boy? Well, according to every news report I'd ever heard back then, it would be considered *molestation*. The concept sounded pretty intriguing to me.

Secret agents were really the ones to blame for making me horny every time I visited Ohio as a teenager. Specifically, it was those dapper, square-jawed spies in the movies, the ones who jetted to impossibly exotic destinations around the globe, checking into posh hotels to sip expensive cocktails with chicly garbed international emissaries. They had adventures. And they had sex. Regardless of gender, they were basically sluts—a word that kids in my school only used for girls, but it seemed to apply just as well to just about any good secret agent on the silver screen. If sex were currency, they'd be truly rich.

At age fourteen, I couldn't make it to Istanbul, Cairo, Berlin, or Moscow. For me, the best potential gateway to a spy-inspired escapade was the octagonal, glass-enclosed lobby of the Cordial Court Motor Inn, a mid-priced, full-service hotel set on the highway-laced outskirts of Ohio's capital. The brand offered all the 1970s glamour you could ask for: giant plastic keychains, a sumptuously vinyl-padded cocktail lounge, and shag carpeting so thick it nearly covered the bottom half of my off-brand sneakers. The hotel had an eight-door stretch limousine that looked like a monstrously overgrown station wagon, and the front parking lot was always filled with the most prestigious vehicles that a Midwesterner like me might want—sumptuously overweight luxury sedans with opera windows, garishly colored sports cars with pinstripes, and sleek coupes with seductive, cat-shaped hood ornaments and covered headlights. It was all so urban and sophisticated, a much-needed break from the small-town predictability that pervaded my hometown. In Columbus, there were no kids to make fun of me, no gym class, and no awkward rides on the school bus. At the hotel, I could invent the identity I wanted, even if only for a few hours.

After a long day staring at endless ribbons of interstate, the sight of the bold hotel logo soaring above Interstate 71 never failed to send my heart racing.

Our visits always started the same. After check-in, if we arrived early enough, my mother and I would relax in the swimming pool area, an activity that consisted of me bobbing around by myself in the water in a baggy swimsuit and wet T-shirt (no, I wasn't entering a wet T-shirt contest; don't you know that redheads burn easily?). My mother would sit nearby in a pecan-toned chaise lounge that matched the color of the hotel's logo, fully clothed in plus-sized cotton/polyester blends from our local Ames discount department store, her head buried in a book (she spent more money on books and education than she did on clothing; she had definite priorities). Sometimes I wished that I had siblings to play with at times like these, but by the time I was an early teenager I was accustomed to hanging out alone.

After I got tired of bobbing (I never did much actual swimming), we'd go back to our clunkily furnished room, accented by a mod swag lamp. My mother would pull back the shiny, vaguely floral covering on her bed and put up her feet. She'd grab the remote control (which was yet another sign we were living lives of luxury, since we didn't have a remote-control TV at home) and switch on the local news. The latest goings-on in Franklin County were of no interest to me, of course, but I was entranced by the splashy intro music, a heart-pumpingly urgent instrumental version of Donna Summer's disco hit "MacArthur Park." I never understood why some kids wore "Disco Sucks" T-shirts at school. For me, the fast-paced synthesizer beat was an irresistible call for me to live the refined urban lifestyle that Ohio's capital surely promised.

Someday I'm going to be an anonymous traveling businessman, staying in luxurious hotels, and living in a big city where all newscasts open with disco music.

I flipped through the airline listings in the Columbus phone book. You could easily tell how cool a city was by the number of airlines that flew there, and Columbus had way more airline service than Rochester.

I'll own a black car with a shiny hood ornament, sit in a hotel lounge where some lady sings "The Look of Love" and brag to fellow guests about everywhere I've been. I'll have my own house—no, an apartment, in a high-rise building like Bob Newhart's in Chicago, but maybe mine will be in Cincinnati since there's a big amusement park nearby and the city's dramatic hills will give me amazing views from the big picture windows in my penthouse.

After the news, my mother would comb her frizzy brown hair and slide into artificial leather mules so we could walk to dinner. When I was younger, our mealtime destination in Columbus was a popular Ohio restaurant chain where we indulged in gloriously heavy biscuits drowned in honey. But in my adolescence, newer and more worldly retail attractions drew us in: the French Market and the Continent, both of which seemed almost exotic enough to impress one of those globetrotting secret agents.

If you really wanted to go to Europe but didn't have the money or your parents wouldn't let you, the next best place was a trip to these two central Ohio retail establishments (at least that's what I thought). The French Market was a supermarket like I'd never seen anywhere else, where you could buy all kinds of expensive foreign food and then sit down and eat it. I could tell the food was foreign because the whole place stank like feet. But hey, maybe that's how Europe smelled, for all I knew. You have to get used to different odors if you're going to be an international globetrotter. After finding the least-smelly dinner we could (perhaps a crusty baguette with cold cuts) we'd wander the Continent, which was billed as a "European-style" shopping village. That meant it had lots of overpriced little stores with multi-paned windows and old-fashioned wooden trim that made you feel like you'd stepped into a holiday display, even in summer.

After a quick loop around the complex, we'd return to our hotel room where my mother would change into a multi-colored polyester nightgown and climb into bed to watch *M*A*S*H* or David Susskind or some other TV show that didn't particularly interest me.

That's when I'd start my secret mission.

"Can I go walk around for a while?" I'd ask innocently.

"Sure, honey, just be careful," she'd say, sipping from an ever-present can of cola. "And don't be gone too long or I'll get worried about you." (I realize that you might wonder why on earth any mother would let her teenage child wander around the Cordial Court Motor Inn alone at night. Well, remember, this was the 1970s, when people weren't quite as aware of the potential perils, and my mother had learned through years of experience that I was too wimpy to be a trouble-maker. She assumed I wouldn't talk to anyone and that I was wise enough to walk away if anyone approached me. She was, perhaps, overly trusting.)

The hotel room door clicking behind me signaled I was in a different world.

Now I'm a secret agent.

I'd promenade confidently across the geometric patterns of the hall carpeting in my approximation of a grown-up businessman, energized by the delicious hotel smell—an intoxicating olfactory cocktail imbued with the most alluring qualities of cleaning supplies, musty carpets, swimming pool chlorine, and cigarette smoke. If someone had bottled that fragrance, I would have bought it and worn it every day to high school.

Gazing into the smoke-filled cocktail lounge, I spied a singer in a low-cut dress, her hair piled high and lips gleaming pink. She might have been one of the women who'd become a formidable adversary for one of those secret agents after he's touched down at some exotic hotel in Rio de Janeiro or Delhi.

I walked away from the lounge, keeping my eyes focused on the serious-faced businessmen who would inevitably walk past me with important-looking briefcases. They all looked the same: white guys with white shirts, dark suits, and ties. I wondered what kind of work they did that allowed them to travel around the country. As far as I was concerned, they were just businessmen. Anonymous businessmen. Anonymous traveling businessmen. A job like that would definitely be cooler than being a long-distance truck driver, which was the career I had dreamed about when I was younger. Sure, I'd get to travel with either type of job. But it's probably more comfortable to drive a luxury sedan with hidden headlamps than a big rig jammed full of frozen biscuits.

Of course, the well-dressed businessmen I passed in the hallway never cast me even a slight glance. I should also note that, while I pictured myself as a suave secret agent, I was a skinny, short, pale boy with flaming red (almost orange) hair, and that I was probably dressed in something along the lines of off-brand, red-piped gym shorts, generic vinyl sneakers, and a T-shirt from one of Ohio's coolest amusement parks. With my stylish sartorial statement and my tight-legged walk that had all the nervous sensuality of a pigeon hurrying to get to a pile of breadcrumbs, I must have stood out like a sore thumb in that hotel. But in my mind, I was where I belonged.

• • •

One of my favorite places to haunt during my night-time hotel expeditions was—surprise, surprise—the men's locker room at the swimming pool. To maximize the amount of time I could spend ogling the older guys—some were as old as thirty-five or forty!—I devised a fool-proof undercover ruse that we shall call, for the purpose of this essay, Operation Lost Stuff.

It was a beautifully simple plan. Basically, I pretended to look for some imaginary object (my swimsuit? my towel? the keys to my luxury coupe? who knows) that I supposedly had left in the locker room. I threw myself into the role, plastering a perplexed look on my face by furrowing my brow and tightening my mouth, then frantically opening random empty lockers and peering inside, shaking my head in frustration as I slammed each door shut. All the while, I'd cast furtive glances at the anonymous traveling businessmen in various stages of undress. My eyes traced the hair on their chests and around their belly buttons as my mind concocted fantastical encounters in which one of them might actually speak to me and invite me to ensconce myself in the velour seats of his glistening, vinyl-roofed coupe with opera windows. We'd probably take a quick spin before returning to the hotel for a frilly drink at the cocktail lounge. Did I want more than cocktails and a car ride? You bet. Actually, I wasn't even interested in alcohol. But what *did* I want? I really wasn't sure.

The *good* thing was that no one paid attention to me in the locker room. The *bad* thing was that no one paid attention to me in the locker room. And the problem with Operation Lost Stuff was that it had a time limit. You can't keep searching forever or you'll blow your cover. After about fifteen minutes, I'd have to head to my next stop: the Continent, where the open-air setting and multiple shops offered plenty of opportunities for intrigue.

The best place to conduct undercover secret agent surveillance at the Continent was the bookshop, where people browsed the magazines that lined one wall. I could easily stand there for quite a while and not attract attention. I'd nonchalantly flick through airplane enthusiast magazines before working up the courage to grab something better: one of those stylish men's magazines that ran racy men's underwear ads in the back. For me, it was the closest thing to porn I'd seen at the time. Every now and then, one of the other men browsing at the magazine rack would look up from reading and scan the shop, but they never seemed to look at me.

Except for that one time when I happened to glance up toward the entrance just as a good-looking, middle-aged man walked in, carrying a gray shopping bag that almost matched the color of his windbreaker. His hair was combed to the side in a perfect good boy style, yet he was a grown-up and his stylish, super neat clothes probably meant he was a businessman during the day. He immediately looked in my direction.

Did that guy just look at me?

He was squinting, smiling ever so slightly, even cocking his head a bit like he was trying to better comprehend my slender masculine beauty.

Maybe he likes my novelty T-shirt.

I shifted my weight from one leg to another and quickly looked down again at the glossy magazine pages, where a muscular blond man was standing splay-legged in the tiniest possible white briefs.

This is no good, I thought. *I can't be looking at this underwear ad. If the guy comes over here, he'll think I'm a weirdo.*

I quickly turned the page. Another sexy guy in his underwear. Darn it. Out of the corner of my eye, I could see the handsome man moving closer, his gaze still fixed in my direction. I needed to be reading something respectable when he arrived, not drooling at bulging underwear. The guy was almost at the magazine rack. I began flicking pages rapidly and with such fervor that the magazine flew out of my hands and onto the tile floor. I bent over to pick it up as quickly as I could.

Darn it, I should have squatted down like a man. I look like one of those drinking bird toys that bobs its head in and out of the glass of water at those roadside gift shops.

I righted myself and assumed as normal a position as possible, which probably involved my hips jutting at an unnatural angle when the guy finally arrived at my side.

"Excuse me," he said.

"Umm, uhh," I look up at him sheepishly, rocking slightly and smiling, being extra careful to smile with my mouth closed since a childhood medication had permanently stained my rather small teeth, making them look like what I affectionately called Victorian-era dead baby dentures.

"Excuse me," he repeated, raising his eyebrows and pointing toward the magazine rack behind me. "Could I just ..."

"Umm, uhh," I repeated, expelling a gush of air that I guess was supposed to pass for a nervous-yet-flirtatious giggle as I stepped out of his way. He reached up, removed a magazine, and quickly left for the checkout counter. He was gone.

Mission aborted. Mister secret agent, you are to report to the home office immediately.

Every mission was aborted in Columbus, actually. Whenever I got back to the hotel room, my mother's hearty snores would be competing with the gunshots ringing from the Quinn Martin crime dramas that were invariably flickering on the TV screen. I'd never wake her up. Instead, I'd creep into the clean white bathroom, close the door, and sit on the cold tile floor. My mind would be filled with visions of anonymous traveling businessmen changing in the locker room. I'd imagine what the hairs on their stomachs must have felt like. And then I'd reach my hand inside my piped shorts to pleasure myself. I'd like to imagine that the world's most famous secret agent might have done the same if he weren't able to find an anonymous traveling spy to keep him company.

24. Trick or Treat

Halloween, October 2014

Halloween parties at an assisted living facility should be fairly predictable. There should be candy. There should be decorations. And some costumes too.

What surprised me the most, however, was the fondling.

But I guess I should be flattered that someone found me as irresistible as a bag full of fresh candy corn.

There was a party for every conceivable occasion at my mother's assisted living residence. Whether it was Christmas, New Year's Eve, or Easter, a giant bowl of tasty, non-alcoholic punch that sat in the facility's luxuriously carpeted lobby accompanied every event.

For Halloween, the facility complemented the neon-colored beverage with a party that was open to residents and employees as well as their families. Staff members were invited to parade their children around the lobby to delight residents with their creative costumes and darling cuteness. It actually sounded like a pleasant way to spend the evening. Plus, after multiple visits during other holidays, I'd become quite fond of the punch, so I looked forward to attending the event.

My mother didn't care much about going, but she felt that the get-togethers were necessary. "Those parties can be so silly," she said as she placed a tiny plastic witch's hat atop her frizzy gray-brown hair. "Some of the old coots living here are a little nutty, but it's a good idea to at least show up and be social for a while." She switched off the TV in her studio apartment and grasped her silver walker as we headed out to the elevator.

Downstairs, golden oldies oozed through the speaker system as we grabbed cups of the all-important punch as well as a small plastic bag of Halloween candy, which was thoughtfully provided by the assisted living facility so that we'd have something to give to the soon-to-arrive little ones.

A crowd of about two dozen seniors had already taken seats around the lobby, leaving us one spot on a heavily cushioned loveseat that was pushed up next to a larger couch, where an elderly gentleman with tousled gray hair sat. Like all the residents, the guy wore what you might call street clothes—in this case, khaki pants, a slightly wrinkled plaid shirt, and a tan windbreaker. He looked like someone you might see shopping in a supermarket or walking down any street. Many of the residents in this assisted living home, in fact, did go out regularly; some had their own cars parked outside.

"Hello, how are you?" I smiled at the man as I sank into the loveseat's silky smoothness.

"I'm fine," he responded, patting my hand on the armrest.

Soon, the front doors swung open, and the giggles of a dozen or so tiny merrymakers filled the lobby. The children excitedly pranced about in a sugar-fueled swirl of energy, stopping at every couch and chair to collect treats from the smiling residents. There was a ballerina and an astronaut. There was a cowboy and a policeman.

And there was a giant hand on my knee.

He must not realize what he's doing, I told myself as I glanced quickly at the gentlemen sitting next to me from the corner of my eye. I scooted my butt slightly across the satiny upholstery toward my mother, slipping my leg away from my friendly neighbor's veiny man paw.

"Isn't she the cutest thing?" my mother said, pointing to a toddler in a tiara and a princess dress.

"She really is a cutie," I said, crossing my legs. "I wonder which princess she's supposed to be?"

"Give her some candy," my mother commanded, handing over the plastic bag. "I won't be able to hear what she says if she talks to me."

As I leaned forward to proffer the finest generic version of Smarties that the facility's money could buy, I noticed, in the corner of my eye, that my neighbor's arm, which lay on the armrest, was slowly turning at the elbow, much like a crane angling above a construction site. Apparently, my leg was the work zone. The lanky limb pivoted, and a warm palm landed gently but firmly on my thigh.

"Oh, Momma, look over there at that little boy!" I blurted gleefully, using my sudden explosion of joy as an excuse to jolt my body skyward, thereby dislodging the wandering hand as I swung myself even closer to my mother. "Is that boy dressed like a miniature Charlie Chaplin? Mussolini? Or Bea Arthur? I can't quite tell!"

"I'm not sure," my mother said, half smiling. I couldn't tell if she'd noticed what was happening.

"Well, I sure do hope that little boy comes over here so we can get a good, good look at him!" I gushed with forced enthusiasm, shaking my leg as I angled my body in the direction of my mother like a teenage girl cozying up to her boyfriend while having a mild epileptic fit. "Are you having a good time, Momma?" I asked, turning my body as sharply as possible in her direction.

"Oh yes, the kids are all very cute," she said, eyeing me a bit strangely as she sipped punch from a plastic cup decorated with a jack-o-lantern sticker.

Why didn't I just say something to the man or get up and move? Well, there was nowhere else to sit. Plus, my mother used a walker, and I couldn't abandon her. I couldn't just suddenly announce that we had to depart immediately. And, since she was hard of hearing, I'd need to explain at such a volume that everyone in the lobby would have heard my plight, possibly resulting in innocent costumed children running in terror to their parents to ask what "being felt up" meant. I didn't want to make a scene. It was easier to just avoid the man's advances.

So now here I was, pretending to admire the costume of every single staff member's child while simultaneously fending off the advances of a large hand that crept toward me like a disembodied body part in some 1950s horror movie. Within minutes, it was back again, arriving at an even higher location on my left thigh. His arm was now fully extended from his couch onto my leg. There was nowhere else to go on the loveseat unless I jumped into my mother's lap.

Okay, I surrender. If feeling me up gives this old man such a thrill, then I'll let him do it. I'm doing my good deed for the day, right? No one's getting hurt. I'm just having my space invaded while providing some Halloween cheer to a frisky senior who probably hasn't gotten laid in a while.

I wondered what real hook-ups would be like in such a tightly monitored environment. Would he tie a sock around the doorknob of his room so that staff would know not to check in on him? Would neighbors gossip if they saw me creeping out of his door late at night with my hair disheveled? Or would they all be asleep?

I leaned back, tossed a piece of candy corn in my mouth, and sighed.

Suddenly, my mother sat up straight.

"I think we've been here long enough," she said firmly, reaching for her walker. "Let's go back upstairs, sweetie. I have some cheese and crackers we can munch on."

I jumped up like I'd just won a prize.

"Happy Halloween everyone!" I called, waving merrily as we left. The man smiled slightly and looked away.

"I told you some of these people are nuts," my mother said as the elevator doors closed behind us.

25. Things My Gay Astrologer Uncle Should Have Warned Me About

The only time I remember seeing my uncle, he rolled his eyes at me. I was about seven years old, and I didn't know much about him. I had no clue that he was a celebrity astrologer. I also didn't know that he was gay, or that I was gay too, for that matter. But looking back now, I wonder: if Don were really as talented a soothsayer as his big-name clients seemed to think, he should have recognized that we had more in common than just our bloodline. And maybe he could have saved me years of confusion as I struggled to figure out who I was.

There was little time for reading the future, apparently, on that summer afternoon in the early 1970s, when our extended family gathered in a sweltering hotel parking lot in Louisville, my mother's hometown. We prepared to disperse into multiple cars to head to a barbecue-and-pancake lunch. Don's fashion-forward attire was proof that he had flown in from his home in New York City; his slim figure was tucked into fashionably tailored shorts and a plaid, short-sleeved shirt with a zipper instead of buttons. He opened his car door with the hand that didn't hold a cigarette and looked at me through thick-framed unisex sunglasses.

"Would you like to ride with me, Mark?"

I looked down at the pavement like an idiot for a few seconds before saying no. "I want to go in Mommy's car." I was a shy kid, and I didn't even remember meeting my uncle Don before; I was too timid to ride with someone I didn't know.

He puffed a long, slow ribbon of smoke into the air. "I should've *known* he'd want to ride with his *mother*," he said to no one in particular.

Why the snotty tone? Why wasn't I worthy of the respectful attention that he lavished on his celebrity client list? Why couldn't he have given me an astrological reading like (I later found out) he regularly gave to Sue Lyon, the actress known for her titular role in *Lolita*, or Lorne Greene, who portrayed the fatherly Ben Cartwright on the TV western *Bonanza*?

If Don had been a good uncle, he would have pulled out his oracle cards right there in the parking lot. He would have lifted me onto the sun-baked trunk of his shiny rental car and said, "Listen kid, I usually charge a lot of money for this, but you're my nephew and you need to know something. The stars are aligned. You're going to be gay like me. Let me set you up with an astrological strategy for success and help you come out to your mother since I've known her longer than you."

But that didn't happen. And by the time I started figuring out who I was, Don was long gone. I don't know if he predicted his own death, but it came early, thanks to the lung cancer brought on by his ever-present cigarettes. By 1972, he had left his star-studded life in New York City and moved to the tiny town of Benton, Kentucky, where he died the following year in the presence of his parents, my grandparents. I don't remember ever seeing him again, and we never had a chance to bond.

Not that we necessarily would have. As far as I can recall, Don never visited our family in western New York State and never timed his trips to Kentucky to coincide with ours except for that one summer vacation. He barely visited Kentucky at all, as far as I knew. Don was, to me, more of an abstract concept than a living, breathing relative. I was more familiar with his glossy, black-and-white publicity photo, which hung in our family room, than I was with him. Don's framed portrait was the only one in our house that looked like a movie star's headshot, with his formal suit and tie, perfectly tilted head, and one arm bent to accommodate the luxuriously long cigarette resting between his fingers. With his elegantly slim face and carefully combed dark hair, he resembled Anthony Perkins in *Psycho*, but in a good way.

Looking back, I understand now why we didn't see Don much. As far as I know, he never came out to his family. Homosexuality wasn't an easy topic in the middle of the twentieth century, and even less for a Southern Baptist family in Kentucky—even if they were educated. I can understand why Don moved to New York City, where at least he had a chance to be himself.

His parents and sisters felt his move to the Big Apple, where he wrote music and plays, was frivolous, even though he'd studied theater at the University of Kentucky and living in New York City tied in with his career goals. If the family didn't approve of his quest to become famous on Broadway, they were downright horrified when, after only moderate success in the theater world, Don found greater fame as a celebrity astrologer. I'm not sure how he ended up being so renowned for his astrology work, but he was. Following the advice of his own readings, he changed his name to Keith and proceeded to take on even more clients. The freshly redubbed Keith Clayton started appearing in national media. David Susskind invited him to talk about "Sex and the Signs of the Zodiac" and Johnny Carson hosted him on *The Tonight Show*. *Life Magazine* interviewed him after he did an astrological reading for Princess Grace and Prince Rainier of Monaco.

You'd think that if national and international media celebrated someone in your family, you'd pore over every appearance. But my mother never called me to the living room to watch her brother on TV, and I didn't see his star-studded press clippings until I happened upon them after his death.

"He was very smart and talented, but he had delusions of grandeur," was about all I could get my mother to say about him.

After my uncle died, my mother and grandparents started referring to him as "poor Don." When I asked why they called him that, my mother said it was because he died young and with credit card debt.

One day when I was in my teens, I rummaged through a giant box of family photos when a black-and-white headshot of a well-dressed young man tumbled out. He looked a little like my uncle, and the portrait had the same movie-star style as Don's publicity photos. I asked my mother who the dashingly dressed gentleman was.

"That was Don's friend," she answered. "They lived together in New York City." She changed the subject quickly, pointing to another old photo and recounting some often-told story about something funny that happened in Louisville. I knew not to ask anything else about the mystery man.

Through all my years growing up, no one ever told me directly that my uncle was gay or that he lived with a "friend." I had to figure it out.

. . .

I have no interest in astrology (or religion), but based on my half-assed research, I discovered that astrologers have viewed homosexuality in varying ways over the years, often depending on the prevailing views of society. The ancient Greek mathematician and astrologer Ptolemy, for example, noted in non-judgmental terms that people can be inclined toward same-sex attraction based on the appearance of signs in their charts. Certain planets—Saturn, Mercury, and Uranus (keep your comments to yourself)—are apparently more associated with queer people.

Beyond those basics, astrology makes my eyes glaze over just as quickly as a church service or a football game. So, without Don's prescient wisdom, I was on my own to navigate my way as the only living gay member of the Chesnut/Clayton clans. But how would I come out? Don had provided no example for me to follow (especially since he never did come out, apparently), and I wasn't sure how my mother would react. If she took the same disapproving stance as she did with her brother, I might end up being as distant as Don, compelled to banish myself from the family, to find solace among the skyscrapers of Manhattan, and to only show up occasionally to creep out younger relatives by offering them a ride in my car.

At least I knew she wouldn't be ashamed of my career choice, whatever that might be. I had no interest in astrology or the theater (and I had no credit card debt, either). Instead, I went away to college in Albany and studied Communications, French, and Spanish. Rather than reading astrological charts, I turned to sociopolitical writings for reassurance about my sexual orientation. I read about the Black civil rights and women's liberation movements and applied those lessons to the plight of gay people. I attended therapy sessions to prepare for the day when I'd finally tell my mother that I was gay. And I was pleasantly surprised by the consistently positive reactions as I came out to my suitemates and friends at college.

For more than a year, I carefully rehearsed my coming-out speech before every visit home. And every single time, I wimped out as soon as I arrived at my mother's house. She didn't ask many questions about my personal life at school, so it was easy to avoid the topic. I made a trial run by coming out to my sister, who was cool about it—although she advised me not to tell our mother, warning that she was too old to understand or accept it.

Which was quite likely true. I had already experienced some of my mother's discomfort after I got my ear pierced during a weekend jaunt to New York City. I was thrilled about the latest enhancement to my finely tuned 1980s New Wave look—until I wrote a letter about it to my mother.

Don't wear the earring around your grandfather, she wrote back. *I know in college things are different, but in Brockport, earrings on a boy mean one thing: GAY.*

That was the first time I'd ever seen her use that word. Those three letters, written in capitals as if they were a biohazard warning, pretty much put the damper on any plans I had to come out anytime soon. I respected her wishes and took out my earring whenever I visited home, so that ended the conversation and there were no more comments. Being gay was so shameful, apparently, that even vague symbols of it must be hidden. If her response to the earring was that strong, I could only imagine how she'd react when I came out. Had my mother evolved since she first dealt with (or, more accurately, avoided) her brother's sexual orientation? I wasn't even completely sure how much of her shame about Don was related to being gay and how much was about being an astrologer. Oh Don, why couldn't you have beamed down some answers from wherever astrologers go after they die?

• • •

I finally worked up my nerve during a holiday visit. My mother and I had just returned from a midnight Christmas Eve service at the Baptist Church. Neither of us was particularly religious by that point—she'd already admitted that she agreed with all the tenets of agnosticism although she couldn't bring herself to embrace the actual term, while I was happily marching down the road to atheism. But hey, there was still something to be said for the holiday season's warm-and-fuzzy sentimentality, so we bundled up and crunched our way through the snow to sing church carols, leaving the rest of the family (my grandfather, my aunt, my sister, her husband, and two children, those heathens!) at home.

The split-level house looked like a middle-class suburban holiday card when we returned, albeit messier than what you'd see on television (in movies, Saint Nicholas didn't usually descend on living rooms where you could barely see the carpeting due to the abundance of furniture, gifts, and books). The glistening lights of the fake Christmas tree pierced the darkness of the living room, and not a soul had stayed awake to welcome us home. My aunt (who was so religious that she refused to attend services at my mother's Northern Baptist church; they were too liberal for her) had retired to her bedroom hours earlier, as had my supposedly earring-hating grandfather. My sister, her husband, and their two young children, who were visiting for the holidays, were asleep in the guest rooms downstairs. This was perhaps my only chance to be alone with my mother during this visit.

She went upstairs and came back down wearing one of her trademark fuzzy bathrobes, a puffed-out creation that looked thick enough to protect her from a nuclear explosion. But would it protect her from my big news? She plopped onto the blue velvet couch, which she draped with a sheet to immunize it from the seasonal onslaught of messy grandchildren, and opened a giant tin canister of multi-flavored popcorn as she clicked on the television.

I sat on the love seat next to the couch and stared at the TV, although I couldn't focus on what was on the screen. My mother tossed wads of popcorn in her mouth and made random, pleasant comments about Christmas and the family. I had no idea what she was saying. I needed to tell her who I was.

If I decided to open my mouth, what would happen? Based on what I'd heard from some kids my age who came out, there could be tears, red faces, hurtful words, slammed doors, and a ruined Christmas vacation, perhaps followed by an early departure back to college in Albany. Coming out never went smoothly. I knew that much.

I couldn't sit still. I went into the kitchen and stood there, gazing pointlessly into the light of the open refrigerator door.

Oh Don, why couldn't you have told me what to expect? You may have never come out to her, but you knew her well enough.

My mother was born in 1925. In Kentucky. To a Southern Baptist family. And even though she had a master's degree, had pretty much given up on organized religion, and extolled the importance of the Black civil rights movement and women's liberation, I never heard her apply that liberal perspective to LGBTQ issues. In fact, I never heard her say a single thing about gay people at all, other than the decidedly negative earring comment. For our family, homosexuality was something you didn't talk about. That's how educated Southern people were; you avoid topics that might make people uncomfortable.

It didn't matter. This had to be done. I gripped the refrigerator door tighter.

"Hey sweetie," she called out, "could you please bring me a pop, with lots of ice?"

"Sure. Um, Mom ..."

"If you don't see any pop in the refrigerator, look out on the steps to the garage. I bought a case yesterday."

"It's okay, Mom, there's plenty of pop in the fridge."

"Thanks sweetie."

"Mom ..."

"What, honey?"

"I have something I really want to tell you. But I don't want you to be worried about it because there's nothing to worry about."

"What is it?"

I swallowed. Trembling hands. Staring at the refrigerator. It felt like my bodily functions might completely shut down.

"I think I'm gay."

A beat of silence. I stared at the white porcelain sink. I looked at the kitchen cabinets.

Say something, Mom.

"Well ... I'm glad that you told me. If that's how you feel, then that's fine. Nothing could ever change my love for you."

And that was it.

That's it? Where's the drama?

I walked into the living room and handed her a fizzing glass of cola. My nerves drove words quickly from my mouth. "I-was-so-nervous-about-telling-you-I-was-afraid-about-how-you'd-react-or-that-you'd-be-worried-and-you-really-don't-need-to-I've-been-doing-so-much-research-about-civil-rights-and-equal-rights-and-how-there-are-so-many-similar-ities-with-the-gay-rights-movement."

My mother lay comfortably on the sofa, one arm behind her head and her gaze alternating between my face and the TV screen.

"There's nothing to worry about at all, sweetie. It's good that you told me." She took a sip from the glass. "Thanks for the pop. Now come sit with me and let's watch some TV before we go to bed. Once the kids are awake tomorrow, we'll be watching the same movies over and over again all day on the VCR."

I don't know why I hadn't predicted this reaction. My mother had a natural Southern avoidance mechanism, designed to avoid conflict at all costs. Better to agree than argue. Better to remain calm than get upset. I was sure that a wave of emotions filled her head and threw her stomach for a loop. But there she was, in her fuzzy bathrobe, calmly sipping her soda pop and shoveling popcorn into her mouth. I made small talk and went to bed.

The holiday was as festive as ever. The aroma of turkey wafted from the kitchen as my niece and nephew tore into their gifts. They giggled at *A Christmas Story*. And neither my mother nor I said a word about our Christmas Eve conversation.

The chilly metal door of a long-distance bus was a welcome sight a few days later. I'd arranged to work full-time for a couple of weeks at the university library during the winter break, so I had to get back early. I watched Rochester fade away as the bus sped toward my new life in Albany. If Don had been around, maybe he could have foreseen what would be the next stage of my relationship with my mother. I sure couldn't.

26. Eunice's Tips for Attending a Funeral

1. Neat, tidy, and respectful is the goal when it comes to funeral attire, but don't overdo it. Black isn't necessary. In fact, dressing too dramatically, as if you were in some movie funeral, may draw unnecessary attention to yourself.
2. Don't be afraid to make small talk. There's no need to be grim the entire time. Pleasant conversation and even a courteous sense of humor can help put people at ease.
3. Maintain a positive tone. Family, friends, and other attendees may feel insecure or uncomfortable, so a well-placed compliment—whether it's about the deceased or the person with whom you're conversi ng, can help keep interactions on a positive track.
4. Don't judge other visitors. If one of your elderly aunts shows up to the funeral in a dirty housecoat and refuses to take it off, embrace her eccentricities and offer her a seat. Let the elders ramble on as much as they like.
5. Avoid religion and politics. Everyone deals with death in their own way, and everyone has their own religious and political beliefs. It's natural for some people to bring up religion during times like this, of course, but you should never project your own beliefs onto someone

else. Likewise, if someone mentions topics that make you feel uncomfortable, it's best to politely excuse yourself and step away. There's no need to offend.

27. Eunice Ignores Her Own Tips for Attending a Funeral

Benton, 1988

My great aunt Bessie Rhea was perplexed. My 1980s New Wave hairdo distracted her so much that she could hardly pay any attention to my grandfather's body, which lay in the casket right in front of her. Instead of gazing at her brother-in-law one last time, she pointed at me from across the funeral home's viewing room.

"Eunice, is that how all the kids in New York cut their hair nowadays?" she asked my mother. "It looks like someone just put a bowl on top of his head and cut right around it."

Since I was several feet away and conversing with another great aunt, I pretended not to hear the booming voice above the hushed murmurs. But I had to admit she was kind of right about my hair, which was carefully crafted to bolster my 1980s fashion sense. My experimental cuts—designed to fit in with the alternative kids at my university—sometimes looked like they'd been executed in the back of a moving pickup truck, and the decidedly severe angles were certainly not a common sight in the funeral homes of western Kentucky.

I turned my attention back to Great Aunt Nancy, who regaled me with tales of her trips to the slaughterhouse to pick up the hard animal fat known as suet. "The birds that fly into our yard just love it," she explained. "They could eat it all day, I can tell you that much."

"I bet you've never fallen face down in your yard, have you?" Bessie Rhea interjected as she ambled quickly over to us, brushing loose curls from her forehead as if she'd just run a race. Her tongue swirled with excitement as she spoke. "I fell real bad one day. Real bad. I went out to the henhouse to get me some eggs and I fell backwards. Well, no sooner'n I got back up, the dog raced in and ate all the chickens. We lost all our chickens that day!"

Funerals generate some of the most interesting conversations. Pop—as everyone in the family called my grandfather—died at age eighty-nine, in March of 1988. He passed away in the hospital where I was born and where my father died, a few minutes from where he'd been living with my mother and aunt. My mother said he spent his final days in bed, deliriously reciting the names of the cities and towns he used to visit as a postal worker in his home state of Kentucky. Unlike when my father died, my mother actually felt it was a good idea to ship my grandfather's remains back to Kentucky since that's where he'd lived for most of his life and all his friends and family were there.

Pop's final resting place would be at Birmingham Cemetery, the graveyard created for a town that no longer existed, except as a nostalgic topic for our older relatives. Named after the eponymous city in England, the town of Birmingham was founded in 1860 on the banks of the Tennessee River in western Kentucky and gradually became the hometown for various generations of my extended family. My relatives spoke glowingly of their time there, but they were forced to move out when the Tennessee Valley Authority, a government economic development agency, announced plans to flood the town out of existence while constructing a massive dam on the Tennessee River in the 1940s. The result was the creation of Kentucky Lake, which for a time was the world's largest artificial lake. Today, most of the recreational boaters who glide across the lake's calm waters are probably unaware that the remnants of a civilization still lie at the bottom.

For some reason, the town of Birmingham didn't choose to relocate in the months before the flooding. But they did relocate the cemetery, including the remains of my ancestors, to a new location in the nearby town of Briensburg. Now, younger generations filled in the unused spaces in the sunsoaked lot. Pop's plot waited for him, next to the space occupied by my grandmother and their celebrity astrologer son Don. My mother had ordered a huge floral arrangement that spelled out *Pop* in white flowers to stand at his burial site. But first came the calling hours and the funeral, for which my mother had written a touching eulogy that I would read (I loved being on stage but was always too lazy to write my own material; luckily, my mother's writing once again saved the day).

• • •

My grandfather's body touched down at the airport in Paducah, western Kentucky's biggest city, on the same chilly winter day that my mother, my aunt, and I drove down from our arriving flight in Louisville. But we didn't see his remains until a couple of days later when we entered the funeral home in Benton.

The calling hours—that's the term we used in the South; I'd only recently learned that Catholics and some other Christians call it a wake—were to take place at a small but attractive funeral home near the big brick town hall and the drug store where I used to order vanilla colas and vanilla phosphates when I was a kid. We entered the funeral home's soothingly pinstriped visitation room, where four indents beneath the wheels of a heavy stand draped in tan fabric marred the perfectly smooth carpeting. On top of that stand was the casket, with Pop's body resting inside.

The metallic coffin reflected the yellow glow of the floor lamps. Pop didn't look like himself. His skin was so flawless that it seemed powdered and glazed (I guess I should find better words to describe this since I just made him sound like a donut). His nose was more pronounced since he wasn't wearing his glasses, and he wasn't smiling or laughing like he usually did.

My mother had put effort into her look, too, donning an attractive, plus-sized skirt and jacket with a light peach color that was complemented by conservatively applied lipstick and makeup. But her father was more gussied up than she was.

• • •

I already knew the routine for calling hours from previous family funerals. My mother passed me peppermints so that no one could tell that we'd had lunch at our favorite local barbecue restaurant, and they clicked in my mouth as my mother and I took turns standing next to the casket and greeting visitors, facing a flurry of perfumed hairspray and the soft, ancient, hands of family friends and kinfolk.

Several people asked if I was married yet. I politely responded in the negative and changed the subject, skillfully shifting to questions about their families, about what was new at the Baptist Church, about the town's most recent Tater Day, an annual celebration that includes food vendors, a flea market, carnival rides, and a demolition derby, or perhaps about the Big Singing, an annual musical event inspired by a nineteenth-century hymnal called *The Southern Harmony and Musical Companion*. I was happy to discuss just about anything to avoid the topic of my personal life. A funeral home in western Kentucky wasn't the right place to come out of the closet to a bunch of random elderly folks. My mother had taught me well to always be agreeable with everyone and avoid any potentially uncomfortable topics, even if that means hiding your own thoughts and opinions.

At one point, I noticed that my grandparents' Southern Baptist minister had cornered my mother near the casket. With his partial comb-over, cheery, wide-lapelled blue blazer, and sizeable tie with bold geometric prints, he looked like he might have been trying to sell high-quality, pre-owned automobiles. I inched my way closer to introduce myself as he touched the sleeve of my mother's peach jacket and smiled.

"Eunice, it's a joyous thing that we will all be reunited with our loved ones in heaven when we pass away. Your father is blessed."

"Thank you very much for saying that," my mother replied, smiling back and nodding noncommittally.

"You understand that, don't you, Eunice? Your father has been reunited with your mother. And you will be together with him again too, someday."

My mother smiled wider. "Well, it gives us great comfort to know that my father believed that," she said, trying to diplomatically let the topic fade as quickly as possible. This guy was an active member of the clergy at the church her parents had attended for decades. She wanted to be respectful. It's what her parents had taught her to do.

Even though she'd never fully renounced her religious beliefs and had taken me to church nearly every Sunday for the first seventeen years of my life, my mother had pretty much stopped believing most of the details of organized religion. She did value the social support that churches provided to people in need, however, and she envied people who had faith. She sometimes felt guilty about her own lack of it. But after years of pondering Christianity, she couldn't bring herself to believe what any minister told her.

This particular preacher seemed unwilling to let her off the hook. His large eyebrows came together as his smile became more purposeful. He was entering full-on Missionary Mode just as my mother was trying to keep her Southern Avoidance Mechanism in the "on" position.

"But ... Eunice ... you *do* believe that we will all be reunited when we join Jesus Christ, don't you? Heaven is waiting for us."

My mother shifted in her open-toed shoes. Losing her father had been difficult, and her patience was growing weak. She raised her eyebrows as her smile took on an artificial glow.

"Well, I can tell you one thing," she said, putting a hand on her hip. "If I die, go to heaven, and see my husband, who hasn't been around since 1969, the first thing he's going to say to me is 'how'd you get so fat?'"

The minister's eyes widened. For a split second, his mouth opened with the beginnings of a confused smile that quickly evaporated. He stayed for a heartbeat more before walking away silently.

And then, as quickly as it had snapped off, the Southern Avoidance Mechanism flicked on again. My mother turned to an elderly woman who stood a few feet away. She smiled warmly and extended her hand. "Thank you so much for coming. Pop would be so happy to know that you're here."

28. I'd Love to See You, But I Don't Want You to See Me

New York City, November 2015

Mountains of greeting cards, nearly all from Brockport, piled up in the weeks before my mother's ninetieth birthday. Glynn, Angel, or I would hold up each card that arrived and announce who'd sent it.

"That's nice," my mother would respond and then look away as we read the contents, as if eavesdropping on the words of a random conversation between strangers in a bus station.

I posted all the cards on the wall behind her bed, a public display that I created partially so that the staff could see how many people loved my mother. She'd used the same reasoning when she used to send cards and letters to her own sister, Rarene, who had moved to a nursing home in California years earlier. "She may not even understand or remember that she's gotten any mail," my mother had said. "But I want the staff to know that there are people who care about her and are keeping an eye on her."

. . .

"How old am I going to be?" my mother asked one day as I taped cards onto the wall.

193

"You're going to be ninety, Momma."

She frowned. "Ninety? *Ninety?* That can't be. That's *old!*"

A couple of days later, after reviewing an especially large number of cards, she turned to me as I sat on her bed. "You know, it's nice that people think to write to me," she said. "But I feel like that part of my life is over."

I appreciated the effort by so many of her friends in Brockport to send greetings. And I felt bad that she wasn't able to write back to any of them. But I had an idea.

"Would you like to dictate a letter to me, and I can send it to all of your friends back home?" I asked.

"I don't know," she said, pausing as she moved one hand from the arm of the wheelchair to her check, in a thinking pose. "I guess that would be the nice thing to do. But I'm not sure what I should say."

"It's okay. We can work on it together." I pulled out a pen and paper from my fake-vintage airline bag. "What would you most like to tell them?"

My mother looked blankly around the solarium where we sat, as if she might find ideas nestled in the leaves of the tiny trees near the window. "Well ... I just don't know."

"Anything special you'd like to ask them?"

Her gaze circled back to me as a grin bubbled up. "Yes. Where the heck am I?"

I chuckled and began writing as my mother continued to dictate. Whenever she stopped, I interjected a few words or asked a question to keep her going. We continued riffing together, egging each other on to be funny. Within a few minutes, we'd come up with a missive that had us both laughing out loud for the first time since her arrival in New York City.

There had been only one other time since my mother started declining that we'd shared a truly healthy laugh. Several months earlier, my mother resided in a rehab center near Brockport to recover from an earlier fall. "I'm just so depressed," she said when I flew up to spend a few days with her at the facility. Try as I might to lighten her mood, nothing made her smile.

Until my husband Angel sent me the remedy.

I had texted him about her inconsolable sadness and my feeling of powerlessness. He responded with a text that contained finely detailed, full-color illustrations of three important world figures: Queen Elizabeth, the Pope, and President Obama. What made the illustrations special, however, was that each of those revered individuals was sitting on a toilet. They were fully dressed from the waist up, but their legs were splayed and open as they did their business on the potty. Those visuals were exactly what my mother needed. She laughed hysterically and repeatedly asked to see them again. She smiled more for the rest of that day.

And now, here we were in New York City crafting our own form of humor. I later decided that the letter was too strange to actually send to her friends. They might not understand the context and might think she'd lost her mind or that I was making fun of her since they weren't present to appreciate the collaborative silliness of the moment. But it was worth every minute of the time we spent putting it together.

Dear Friends,

The only sensible question I can ask is "Where am I?" I'm not sure of the answer, but maybe one of you can fill me in. I do remember you as very, very good friends, and I was lucky to have you. Now, I suppose I am lucky just to be alive. Maybe not so lucky. But we must play with the cards we are dealt.

I will be ninety this fall.

Glynn and Mark are very loyal to me, and I see them as often as possible.

Venerable Hills is a nice facility with two people in each room, but I don't even remember who my roommate is.

Wait, what did I just say?

How will I remember to mail this letter?

Letter? What letter?

Life is so sad.

Love you all and thinking of you. How many of you are there, anyway? I'd love to see you, but I don't want you to see me!

In closing ... where's the bathroom?

Love,

Eunice

29. Trip Whore: A Ten-Point Plan to Become a Travel Writer

If you ask fifty people to name their idea of a dream job, at least one of them will probably say "travel writer." I'm one of those people. Who wouldn't want to get paid to travel around the world and enjoy free stays in luxurious hotels, international delicacies, and visits to world-famous tourist sites?

Actually, *most* people wouldn't want the job when it comes right down to it because most people wouldn't want to earn legendarily low writer's wages, even as they enjoy the magnificently glamorous perks. (I supplement my travel writing with copywriting, branded content, and consulting for travel industry clients. But that's another story.)

I created this ten-point plan for those who *do* suffer from a wanderlust more powerful than their common sense. It's those daydreamers who sometimes ask me how I got into this career.

The truth is, I don't really know the best path to become a travel writer. I never followed some strategic, pre-determined route to get to where I am now. I just followed my passion. After graduating from college, it took me about eight years to gradually steer my career toward the prestigious halls of the nation's leading travel trade publisher. Once I was there, things started to fall into place (even after I was laid off).

So, for those of you who long for a life on the road, here are the steps that I took. You can ignore any details that don't apply to you.

1. Study whatever you want in college. And get drunk too. Maybe get a New Wave haircut and wear eye shadow on your lips.

Oh sure, a fancy degree in journalism or creative writing would be a great idea if you want to be a travel writer. But you don't really need a specialized education to be a writer. You just need to write well, get your point across, and understand the industry. I had no specific goals when I enrolled at the State University of New York at Albany—aside from spinning tunes as the DJ of Club 91, a weekly dance music show on the university's radio station, where the synthesizer-driven beats got me pumped up for drunken nights out at Albany's hottest New Wave clubs. I did my best to look the part, with thrift-store clothing, heaps of black eyeliner, and naturally red hair that I sometimes enhanced with various shades of blond, either combed down to cover one eye or sprayed up with so much cheap hairspray that even a hurricane couldn't have moved it. I also found that green eye shadow made an especially stylish fashion statement when applied to the lips. My makeup even stayed on when I got so drunk that I fell asleep in a snowbank outside of a dance club called 288. Luckily, my friends found me, woke me up, and escorted me home.

What does all of this have to do with my formation as a travel writer? Nothing. But it's all I can tell you about my college years. I guess I should mention that I did work in the library throughout my time in Albany too, although that doesn't have anything to do with my eventual career, either. I even studied a bit and got decent grades (the State University of New York is an admirable institution, by the way, and supposedly the largest network of universities and colleges in the United States; my mother and sister both got degrees from SUNY Brockport and my father taught there, so you could say we're a SUNY family). But my area of study wasn't related to what I do now: I had a major in Communications with French and Spanish minors (read that out loud and it sounds like I was learning how to converse with mine workers in France and Spain).

2. Move to where the work is, even if it's only because your mother doesn't want you to come out to your grandfather.

Since being a travel writer involves travel, you'd think that it wouldn't really matter where you live. But it actually does. There are two reasons for this: one, if you want a permanent, full-time job with one company, you may need to be where that employer is located (unless they allow telecommuting). Two, if you're freelancing and plan to take press trips, you need to be somewhere that's fairly well connected by air to far-off destinations.

I didn't have travel writing in mind when I was in college, so I wasn't thinking about any of this when graduation approached. But I did want to live in a big city since I wanted something different from my small-town upbringing. My options were limited since I had no jobs lined up and no real money saved as graduation quickly approached. I realized that I needed a place to live for free until I could find a viable source of income. Maybe moving back home to Brockport would make sense, if only for a while.

Or maybe not, as I discovered during one definitive phone call with my mother. As usual, I still tried to keep lines of communication open to talk about the fact that I was gay, and I thought that eventually, more people in our family should know. After all, being gay isn't a bad thing, right?

"I know it may be weird to talk about my sexual orientation with Pop and Rarene," I told my mother, referring to my grandfather and aunt, both of whom lived with her. "I just want you to know that you can decide when you think is the best time to let them know that I'm gay. I'll follow your lead."

"If you were going to live here with us after you graduate, then we would deal with that," she answered calmly. "But since I know the last thing on earth you want is to move home, then there's no reason for them to know." Case closed. She hadn't even asked me if I *wanted* to move back, or if I wanted to come out to the rest of the family. I didn't know how to respond, so I changed the subject to some boring topic like how many Buffalo wings I'd eaten that weekend.

Half of her statement was on target, I have to admit. I really didn't want to move back in with my family. I was considering it only because I was broke and had no post-graduation job. At any rate, my mother helped to obliterate any doubts I might have had. It was a bit harsh, but what could I do? I'd already sent her books and magazine articles about how parents can deal with having a gay kid, and her response was always radio silence.

Her attitude, to be honest, pushed me to be independent and do what was best for my own mental health: to go out into the world on my own. The end result was positive.

Still, I needed psychological support. A university psychotherapist helped me to confront the three overarching issues that vexed me during my senior year: my graduation and career anxiety, my mother's unwillingness to talk about homosexuality, and the breakup of a disastrous relationship with my first-ever boyfriend (we'll have to deal with that in another essay; it would be too distracting now to bring up the beautiful boy I dated who unintentionally looked like a young Lana Turner. See? You're already distracted and trying to picture what he looked like. Unless you don't know who Lana Turner is, which is quite likely).

In spite of my mother's reticence about fully accepting my sexual orientation, she still managed to be warm in other ways during my final year of college. She even bought me my first (and so far, only) car as an early graduation gift: a spiffy little used sports car, in the same maroon color as my grandfather's long-gone luxury sedan. I called my car the DiscoLiner to reflect my love of dance music.

As it turned out, I didn't have to look too hard to find a post-graduation crash pad. My salvation came from one of my best high school friends, who was confusingly named Mark too (he was the same guy who as a teenager had coveted the name-brand cookies and other name-brand snack food that my mother used to buy me). Mark had moved to New York City several months before my graduation, and he offered to let me sleep in his living room in Brooklyn, rent-free, until I found work.

3. Find a job that's somewhat related to what you really want to do—preferably, one that allows you to commit aviation fraud.

Few people land their dream job right away. Like many recent graduates, I made frequent job changes in my early years. Only a couple had travel benefits, but first I had to suffer through an excruciating job as an "executive assistant" to a high-ranking director at a major cosmetics company, which sounds glamorous but mostly involved arranging magazines and a water pitcher *just so* before he arrived every morning to his corner office, then fetching his dry cleaning and occasionally chatting by phone with a mildly famous celebrity who'd lent her name to a line of fragrances. It was all a bit like *The Devil Wears Prada*, but less interesting. (I also accidentally ate dog poop on a croissant while I worked there, but that's one more story that must wait for another time.)

Much better was my job as an editor at a small medical publisher, which provided the unexpected opportunity to fly free by committing aviation fraud. It was an idea hatched and proposed by the company's president. After noticing the airline memorabilia that decorated my cubicle, he realized that I was a travel addict and decided that I could help him maintain his elite frequent flyer status with a now-defunct airline that was one of the world's most legendary carriers at the time. He asked me if I'd like to fly an annual mileage run to California so that he could keep his elite status.

To do this, I had to assume his identity, which was much easier than you might think. Back in the late 1980s and early 1990s, believe it or not, airlines didn't yet ask passengers for identification at the airport. I could just march my twenty-four-year-old butt up to the ticket counter at JFK, glide through security, and strut effortlessly aboard a glistening, Los Angeles-bound jumbo jet, all using the name of a fifty-something businessman. It was disorienting at first to hear the staff address me by someone else's name, but I got used to it quickly. I'd do just about anything to fly for free.

4. Build your personal route map.

We all have route maps, even if most people never document them. A route map is a diagram of everywhere you've been—whether by plane, car, or even by foot. We've all traveled somewhere, even if it's just to the neighboring town to buy porn as a teenager (okay, maybe that was just me). Whatever the map looks like, where you've been says something about who you are.

I got hooked on travel so young that I started drawing my own personal route map in middle school, and I updated it every time I flew a new route. The point is, if you're interested in becoming a professional travel writer, it's not a bad idea to follow your passion now and start exploring the world, even if it's on your own and even if you're not traveling far from home.

You don't need to be rich to travel. I didn't have much time or money to travel when I was in my twenties, but I squeezed maximum value out of every opportunity. And even though I wasn't writing articles for any magazines yet, I took notes, wrote journals, and snapped photos to document every important moment. It was instinctual. I didn't want to forget a thing about any journey I took.

I taught myself how to work the system. A key part of this involved learning the fine art of being bumped from a flight.

During trips back to see my family, I aimed to be the first person to volunteer my seat and get bumped when flights were oversold. Depending on the airline, that got me either a free domestic round-trip or a cash voucher. I used those credits to visit San Francisco, New Orleans, Los Angeles, and San Diego.

Frequent flyer miles are another important tool for anyone obsessed with travel. I hoarded miles and scoped out irresistible deals. One of my biggest coups was using a triple-mile promotion on a $250 round-trip ticket from Newark to London Gatwick, which produced enough frequent flyer mileage for a free ticket to Buenos Aires. Between 1987 and 1991 (all while I was in my early twenties), I added England, Holland, Argentina, the Dominican Republic, Puerto Rico, and Mexico to my international route map. Not bad for a kid just out of school whose salary had only risen from $12,000 to $25,000 a year.

5. Get media attention—even if you're not really newsworthy.

An easy way to dip your toes into travel journalism is to inject yourself into the news. One thing to note: It's not easy to get a TV reporter to notice you when you're one of hundreds standing outside of an airport terminal. Back in 1989, I had to stare at one of television journalism's biggest rising stars for about ten minutes before she even looked at me. I was just a face in the crowd, standing in a seemingly endless line outside of New York's LaGuardia airport on a chilly day in 1989. Hundreds of people had gathered, eager to pay the ridiculously low fare of $12 to board a shuttle flight to Boston or Washington, D.C.

The cheap tickets—and the national news coverage—were all because this particular airline was desperately trying to attract passengers back during a crippling strike. The flash sale even included bonus frequent flyer mileage.

I knew it was wrong to cross the unions' picket line. But the trip. The mileage. I was young and poor and desperate to travel. So I donned my psychological and moral blinders and walked straight into that overcrowded terminal with a crisp $20 bill in hand. And when I saw that up-and-coming reporter, I wanted her to document my transgression.

I could have hidden from the cameras. But no, this was my big chance to be on the national news. Years earlier, a TV reporter interviewed me in front of Greater Buffalo International Airport after J.J., Kenny, and I had slept all night on the outside sidewalk in order to get a twenty-nine-cent promotional fare on New York Air (yes, twenty-nine cents, and yes, our parents were permissive enough to let their teenage sons fly all the way to New York City and stay unchaperoned in a hotel).

An interview on a national newscast would take me to the next level. Eventually, the famed reporter did approach me for a one-line sound bite, which I completely flubbed because her sophisticated, international speech patterns made me so self-conscious of my Great Lakes accent that I tried to answer her with the same high-class vocal intonation. Instead, I sounded like an extraterrestrial who'd just learned English. She disappeared before I had time to do a makeover, leaving me to hop aboard a shiny jet on my next adventure.

If you don't find yourself in front of a camera talking like an idiot with a fake accent, it's probably best to just follow a more professional path, as highlighted in the next step.

6. Use freelance work and personal projects to steer your full-time career in new directions.

I didn't know exactly where I should be working, but I knew what I liked: being creative, writing, and traveling. So I decided to follow my passions and see where they led.

I enjoyed my jobs, but I knew there was something better out there. I began using freelance endeavors and personal projects to steer myself toward a more rewarding future.

To prove my ability as a travel writer, I took on small free-lance assignments that would result in writing clips that I could then show to other publishers. I began by writing a monthly travel column—with no pay—for a tiny monthly newspaper that was distributed for free in Greenwich Village. Then I founded a fanzine (there were no websites or blogs back then) called *Skyjack Magazine*, which was dedicated to "gay people who fly." For *Skyjack*, I wrote and published off-the-wall articles and interviews with flight attendants, pilots, and snarky LGBTQ travelers who reveled in the campy aspects of the airline industry (one of *Skyjack*'s ongoing columns was "More Movies the Airlines Won't Show You," which provided tongue-in-cheek reviews of bad airline disaster movies and other films that celebrated over-the-top images of air travel). Believe it or not, I actually made money on *Skyjack*, attracting paying subscribers and even an investor who bought the publication and then paid me to stay on as the part-time editor for several years.

7. Don't ever give up.

You've got to keep on going. That's good advice for any career or goal.

If I'd given up, I wouldn't have become a travel writer. For months, I scanned the want ads and applied for any full-time job I could find in travel publishing. One particular employer kept popping up in the listings. The company, which owned a variety of top travel industry publications, sounded like the perfect place for me. The only downside: the office was in suburban New Jersey, which required a bus ride from my home in Manhattan. But passion outweighs practicality, so I applied for an editorial job there and got an interview.

They didn't hire me.

A few weeks later, I applied again for another job, in a different division of the same company. I got an interview.

They didn't hire me.

I tried a third time with yet another division. Still no offer. And yet those help wanted ads from the Garden State kept appearing, enticing me.

I decided to give it one last shot. The human resources guy seemed to like me enough to keep showing my résumé around the company, so it would be silly not to keep trying. Luckily for me, the fourth time was the charm. After just one interview with the department head, the company hired me as an assistant editor in the custom publishing department. I have a wonderful woman named Jane to thank for giving me my first shot in that career path.

Custom publishing is different from journalism. It's an editorial hybrid that goes by many names—branded content, sponsored content, or strategic content, for example. But they all pretty much mean the same thing: advertorial content, created in cahoots with a sponsor who pays big bucks for promotional material that's good enough to attract attention and engage readers. I was finally writing about the travel industry. It was spectacular. During my time in that position, I wrote and edited copy for clients ranging from tourism offices to hotel chains and airlines. After just a couple months, my boss sent me on my first press trip. I was in heaven.

That work prepared me for another position, within the same company, that involved travel on a regular basis—thanks to another wonderful manager, Claudette, who hired me to become her Caribbean editor. Throughout those years, I never stopped freelance writing, either; I even found time to write an entire book called *The Gay Vacation Guide: The Best Trips and How to Plan Them.*

8. Learn how to fake it.

You may think travel writing is all glamour, but if you're a serious travel writer and editor (especially if you work for travel industry publications rather than consumer outlets), you must also be able to comprehend complex industry issues, and sometimes pretend you're interested in less-than-fascinating topics. Trade publications are produced for people who work in the industry—travel agents, tour operators, hoteliers, meeting planners—and they require close attention to the nuts and bolts of the industry. Average travel enthusiasts might find some of it a bit dull. But you need to understand your readers (even when their interests are different from yours) and make everything compelling, relatable, and useful. Flexible meeting space? Fascinating. Hotel cleaning protocols? Love it. Airline codeshares? Nothing better in this world.

You'll also need to master the concept of the press trip, those legendary junkets that take reporters off to the far reaches of the world.

To outsiders, press trips might look like a free vacation. You're flown to an exciting destination, checked into a luxurious hotel, fed gourmet cuisine, and toured around like a VIP. Friends, family, and followers only see your photos of lush swimming pools, shimmering beaches, and posh accommodations, so they could easily assume that you're spending every day lazing on a lounge chair and sipping piña coladas. What most people don't realize is that travel writers often don't have time to dip their toes into the pool or lie back on the beach. Meetings and interviews with hotel and tourism officials often fill our days, as well as site inspections and tours that sometimes require participants to "ooh" and "ahh" over meeting rooms and half-built construction sites. Press trip schedules can sometimes be tiring, too, with early-morning wake-up calls and late-night dinners that last way longer than you'd like with people who may not be your first choice as dining companions. But in my opinion, it's an exciting learning experience and it's worth every minute.

9. Learn how to meet—and insult—celebrities.

When you're a travel writer, if you're lucky, you might even meet the occasional celebrity. I've shaken hands with Sidney

Poitier, conversed with presidents of several Latin American countries, and kissed the cheek of Mexico's former first lady.

Meeting celebrities is even more memorable when you accidentally insult them. At the grand opening party of a lavish resort in the Bahamas, for example, I failed to recognize a 1970s pop star and repeatedly asked him to get out of the way as I tried to take photos. I thought he was some random hotel guest.

"You want me in the picture too," he assured me.

"No, I don't, but thanks!" I said, laughing politely as I waved him away. Repeatedly.

He still didn't move. He even told me who he was. I looked closer and suddenly recognized the eyes, the smile, the slimmer man inside. It really was him. I apologized profusely and took the photo. He was gracious about my mistake. "It happens all the time," he said.

The point is, you should be happy when you get the chance to meet people of all backgrounds, and travel writing is a great way to do so—even if sometimes you don't realize who you're talking to.

10. Commit to being a trip whore.

If you're passionate about being a travel writer, prepare to be called a trip whore. But don't misunderstand. The term doesn't mean that you have sex everywhere you go (although if you were truly following in the footsteps of some secret agents, you might).

Being a trip whore just means that you don't know how to say no to a free trip.

I first learned the term when I started working for that travel trade publisher in 1994. The moniker seemed perfect for me.

I was ready to go just about anywhere. After all, I'd spent years building a career centered around my passion. Writing and editing were the only things I did fairly well, and traveling was, well, the most important thing in life, so why would you ever turn down a trip? (Oh yeah, my husband, family, friends, and other loved ones were more important, for sure. That's what I meant to say. The intoxicating aroma of jet fuel that blew in from the tarmac at the airport temporarily clouded my mind as I wrote this).

30. Five Blurry Phases

At what point do you give up and move on? At what point do you accept a person's imperfections and just appreciate what you've got without pushing for more?

I recently came across a survey from the United Kingdom that found twenty-five percent of parents were "desperately" disappointed with their adult children. The reasons why parents become disillusioned with their grown-up kids, according to another report, runs the gamut from perceiving them as lazy to thinking they've made bad life choices. Being vegan and going to jail also appeared on the list. If your kid were both vegan *and* an inmate, I guess you should just totally throw in the towel.

I came across this information not because I was looking for it (although I'm sure my mother had reasons to be disappointed in me, plenty of times). I was trying to research the opposite: why adult kids might be disappointed in their parents. But I found almost nothing. No statistics, no lists of complaints.

No wonder it took me decades of observation, negotiation, and meditation to navigate my frustration with the winding, imperfect path my mother followed toward dealing with the fact that I was gay. Every LGBTQ person who comes out to their parents has a unique story, of course. I can sum up my mother's path toward acceptance in five decidedly blurry phases.

Phase 1: Passive agreement and silence

After I came out to my mother in the mid-1980s, she never asked me a single question about my sexual orientation. For years. Needless to say, she wasn't eager to ask about my love life, either. Our mother-son relationship was absolutely fine in all other regards. We got along well whenever I went home to visit from college or from my post-college home in New York City. We spoke by phone two or three times a month, saw each other for all major holidays, and had cheerful conversations. But it was up to me to bring up the fact that I was queer, and when I did, she changed the topic quickly.

It's not like I hadn't tried to educate her over the years about the modern realities of being gay. The late twentieth century was a far cry from the closeted, shame-filled decades when my uncle Don was living with his "friend" in New York City. Oh, how I tried to tell her that. I wrote long letters about the Gay Rights Movement. I sent magazine articles that quoted psychologists, psychiatrists, health experts, and politicians about how homosexuality is natural. I talked about my participation in gay rights demonstrations and events, and my volunteer work. I drew parallels between the civil rights struggles of LGBTQ people, women, and African Americans since she supported the latter two wholeheartedly and was an educated, liberal woman with a master's degree in history. I'm sure I imbued my communiques with all the heavy-handed righteousness and urgency of my youth. But I felt it was necessary because even with that approach, her response generally consisted of letters about her work as a historian and questions about my job in New York City. Never a word about the gay stuff.

Once, I mailed my mother a much-praised book called *Now That You Know: What Every Parent Should Know About Homosexuality*, accompanied by a letter in which I mustered up all the common sense I could. Here's what I wrote:

I remember when I was a kid you brought home a book from the library that was all about where babies come from. It was perfect timing because it was just about when I was beginning to have questions about that sort of stuff—and I guess you knew because I think I had asked you a few questions. Well, it's been about five years since I told you that I'm gay, and although you haven't really asked me any questions, I've assumed that you must have some, or some concerns may have arisen. And that's why, just like when you brought that book home for me, I thought it would be good to get that book Now That You Know *for you.*

I realize that it's been hard for us to discuss this matter. I want you to also realize that I am always willing to answer any questions or concerns you have. I know that you have experienced some negative feelings about me, based on how society has educated you about homosexuality. Well, one option we as individuals have is to re-educate ourselves as we see fit, to examine stereotypes and fears we hold, and to remove them from our minds and replace them with reality.

A week or so later, I followed up with a phone call.
"Did you get the package I sent?"
"Oh yes, I got it."
"I hope you have a chance to read some of that book. I thought it might help you."
"Oh yes, I will. It looks very interesting. Thank you."
And then, before I knew it, we were talking about work. Or the latest movies we'd seen. Or the weather. Something. Anything but my gayness. I didn't know what to do about her reluctance to talk. Maybe I was feeling the same way that she did when she dutifully brought me that library book about sex, oh so many years ago. I never even opened it and never said a thing about it to her. I was embarrassed and uncomfortable. And I guess she felt the same way now.

• • •

When it came to discussing my romantic life, I had to think like a public relations executive. Any mention to my mother about relationships had to be in the form of slickly packaged, decidedly positive scenarios. I was afraid that any failed relationship would reinforce her negative feelings about homosexuality and confirm that I was doomed to spend my life alone. I had three serious boyfriends before I met Angel, but only mentioned one to my mother, and only after we'd been together for more than a year. After I met Angel (during a drunken evening out at Limelight, a legendary church-turned-nightclub in New York City), I didn't say a thing to my mother until Angel and I had passed the one-year anniversary and planned to move in together. It was time for her to know. But I needed the right moment.

"What are you doing this weekend, sweetie?" she asked during one of our semi-weekly phone calls. "Anything fun?"

That was my opportunity.

"Well, I'm dating a really nice guy named Angel. He works for an advertising agency and lives in Manhattan, on the Upper East Side. We're going to see a show this weekend, an off-Broadway show that's supposed to be good." Maybe it was dumb of me, but I knew I needed to give her an out—a topic she could latch onto that would allow her to politely continue the conversation without directly addressing my relationship. She picked up on it right away.

"That sounds like fun, sweetie. What's the show about?"

No questions about Angel. But at least it was a start.

A few months later, I told her that we were registering as domestic partners with the New York City government, which would provide us with some of the legal benefits of marriage (this was 1993, and there was no same-sex marriage). Her reaction was similarly pleasant and noncommittal.

"Well, then that sounds like a very good idea. That's nice, sweetie."

No questions, no gushing support. I asked my sister to be the one to "officially" proclaim the news of our partnership in an announcement we mailed to friends and family.

Phase 2: Inviting the boyfriend

Just as mothers gently push their children to learn new things as they grow up, children sometimes need to prod their parents a bit too. This was especially important once I was in a serious relationship.

"You know Momma, Angel and I are a couple now, and I would hate to have to miss out on a holiday with my family someday because I can't bring him up to Brockport," I told my mother during one visit.

"Well, of course Angel is welcome to come up with you any time," she responded.

A few months later, Angel and I found ourselves in the bustling terminal at LaGuardia Airport, ready to board a flight to Rochester.

Phase 3: Getting charmed by the boyfriend

During that first visit, Angel's warm personality and politeness seemed to charm my mother and aunt, who still lived with her. He washed dishes. He held doors open. He talked with my mother about recipes. He asked about my childhood. He bought cedar chips to refurbish the garden in front of her house. And he laughed politely when we reverted to endless family stories while sitting around the dinner table.

After that first successful visit, Angel began accompanying me to Brockport twice a year, usually for Christmas and the Fourth of July (for which my mother spearheaded a town celebration hosted by the historical society where she worked). Whenever we visited together, my mother stocked the refrigerator with shrimp and beer because she knew Angel liked them. It was a lovely gesture.

Angel's presence seemed to relax my mother. It was easier for her to embrace me being gay if it involved an actual human—and a nice one, at that—rather than her grappling with an intangible concept that she'd been raised to think of as a one-way ticket to loneliness (I'd say hell, but by then she no longer believed in heaven or hell). She often gave him more Christmas presents than she did to me; her gifts were usually inexpensive and practical items, but that was okay. One year, she gave Angel a vintage Puerto Rican cookbook that she'd found at a used book sale; it just happened to be the same title that Angel's parents had received as a wedding gift, decades earlier.

Angel opened that gift while sitting on the same couch where my mother had been resting when I came out to her years earlier, a few feet from the same fake Christmas tree that had stood silently as I made my dramatic revelation. Times do change.

Phase 4: Freaking out about the wedding

Angel and I got married in 2014. Not for particularly romantic or traditional reasons; we'd already been together for twenty-three years and didn't need societal acceptance or a religious blessing. Plus, we both hated weddings. The fancy outfits, the long ceremonies, the giant guest lists, the religious theatrics, the huge cost for something that's over in a matter of hours … ugh. We'd rather have spent that money on a good vacation. But we wanted the legal benefits of marriage. Not having to pay exorbitant taxes on an inheritance, for example, was reason enough to tie the knot.

Angel wanted the most bare-bones ceremony possible, with no celebration. But I had a slightly bigger idea. I thought it would be nice to share the experience with my mother, especially since we hadn't been able to celebrate our domestic partnership with her. Now, she was comfortable with Angel and had spent time with him. Plus, I found the coolest possible place to get married: Greater Rochester International Airport, a sleek, glassy terminal with a small, stylishly minimalist chapel just a few steps from the thumping baggage claim. I verified that the chapel was available for wedding ceremonies. It seemed so perfect: Angel and I both loved to travel, and what better way to celebrate our union than on the grounds where my addiction to air travel first took hold, and in the presence of the woman who gave me my travel bug? My mother had come to accept and love Angel. The time and the location were perfect.

After getting Angel's approval and contacting the airport, I excitedly called my mother. Her reaction seemed, well, nervous.

"They allow weddings at the airport?" she asked. "How will you get permission to use the chapel? I'm not sure who we would invite. I'm not sure who would come to the ceremony." I suggested a few of her closest friends, who were liberal, educated, and already knew Angel. They'd had us all over for multiple dinners. It would be fun to have some of them attend the wedding, and then join us for a celebratory lunch; we'd even found a restaurant that specialized in same-sex wedding events.

"I'm not sure if my friends would feel comfortable." Okay, so maybe no friends, just her. "Well, if it's what you want to do," she answered. Not the most enthusiastic response.

I decided to move forward anyway, beginning my search for someone who could lead the ceremony and started floating dates. Then my sister called one day. She'd been discussing the situation with her husband, Mike.

"I've been talking to Granny," she said, using the term that everyone in our immediate family—except me—now used to refer to my mother. "She's a nervous wreck, worrying about who's going to go to the ceremony. Mike and I both strongly feel that you should cancel your plans to get married in Rochester." Her word choice sounded like it was a decision made by the board of directors of some corporation.

I shed tears of frustration as I told Angel that we'd have to drop our plans.

"What the fuck do I have to do to get her to be normal about this?" I asked him. "All I want to do is get married."

"This sucks," Angel confirmed, putting his arms around me. "But you know what? She's an older woman and there's nothing we can do about it. This is how she feels, even though we know her friends would be cool about it. It's easier to just move on instead of torturing yourself more. Call Granny and don't say anything about her freaking out. Just tell her that we've decided it would be easier to get married in New York City. You can say that we'll go up to Rochester later and we can just have a lunch to celebrate, but just with her."

Angel was always a master at providing logical solutions to complex issues. I called my mother and used his script.

"That sounds fine," she answered cheerily. "I'll look forward to seeing you both when you come up. We'll have a *big time*." Her tone was light, without a hint of unease. She didn't ask why we changed plans.

Phase 5: Giving a great gift

Just before our wedding day, a card arrived from my mother. *You two have brought much happiness to me, and I hope you will continue to be happy together forever,* she wrote. A check for $1,000 tumbled out—a significant sum for an older woman with a small income.

My mother wasn't perfect, and neither was I. She wasn't able to go as far as I'd hoped to feel comfortable with my identity, but she always treated me with respect and did as much as she could. I'm sure I was not the perfect son she might have wished for, either. At some point, you've got to accept and appreciate what you've got.

My sister served as the witness when Angel and I tied the knot at the marriage license bureau in Manhattan. We used some of my mother's gift money to pay for a celebratory lunch in New York City, and the rest went toward a wonderful honeymoon in Barcelona. The following month, when Angel and I visited Brockport, my mother took us out for a celebratory lunch in Rochester. She let us choose the venue, a restaurant where we'd originally planned to have our post-wedding dinner. It was a lovely spring day, and the icicles had melted.

31. Eunice's Tips for Dealing with Situations That Suck

1. Look for the silver lining. If your husband dies, make the most of your new freedom. Go back to school, get an undergraduate degree. Then get a graduate degree. Launch a new career. Follow your dreams and your passions.
2. Be a martyr. If your parents stay with you for too long and you don't have time to get your own hair cut because you're too busy taking your elderly mother to the beauty parlor every damned week, lock yourself in the bathroom with a pair of pinking shears and give yourself a jagged, insane-looking haircut that will truly make a statement not only about fashion but also about the negative effects of too much family togetherness.
3. Make it funny. When you get to a point where you know you're losing control of your life, both physically and mentally, a smile and a well-placed joke or two can bring levity to the moment, both for you and those around you. And no matter what's happening, remember the centuries-old Persian refrain, "this too shall pass." Of course, gas passes, too.
4. Do what you have to do. If you're left as the only person to raise a sometimes-difficult son or pull your elderly father out of his depression after your mother dies, or your son

comes out of the closet, don't overthink your situation. Don't waste time feeling sorry for yourself. Just do what you have to do.

32. Better That I Didn't Remember

New York City, November 2015

My cell phone rang late one night as Angel and I were about to hear some predictable verdict on a long-running cop show.

"Your mother's very upset," the nurse said. "Is there any way you could come to see her now?"

Tall, barren trees cast dramatic shadows against the brick apartment buildings near the nursing home, reminding me of the cloaked silhouettes of film noir villains following some unknowing victim.

This was the first time I'd been inside the nursing home after visiting hours. The lights shone just as jarringly bright as always. But the building was nearly silent, as if the residents had evacuated suddenly but someone forgot to turn off the lights. There were no televisions blaring, no equipment rattling, no residents sitting in the second-floor hallways or lounges—except for my mother, who sobbed silently in her wheelchair, which the aide had parked in the sunroom. Her hair was disheveled, and she wasn't wearing her glasses, I assumed because she'd been in bed. Her sleeping clothes looked like a wrinkled surgical smock.

"Oh thank god," she said, grabbing my hand with force as I knelt next to her wheelchair. "I've been ... so worried ..."

"What's wrong, Momma?"

"Someone died!" Her eyes widened in horror.

"Who?"

"I'm not sure," she said, tightening her grip on my fingers. "I was so scared it was you or Glynn."

"Well, I'm here and I'm okay, and I spoke with Glynn earlier today," I said, putting my free arm around her shoulder. "She's at home in New Jersey, so I know that she's fine too. Don't worry."

"But I know *for sure* that someone died." She frowned, nodding her head with certainty.

"What makes you think that?"

"I don't even remember how I know, but I know."

"Well, it's possible that someone *did* pass away, Momma. But no one has died that I know of, so it's not anyone in our family. Maybe you had a bad dream. But I will try to find out. Just don't worry about Glynn and me, all right? Everyone in the family is okay."

"Well, that's a relief," she answered, her chest sinking as she let out a long sigh. "I'm so glad to see you. I really was afraid you were dead!"

"Well, you're stuck with me for a while longer, Momma." I smiled and changed the subject to more mundane topics like bad nursing home food and fierce winter weather forecasts. Once she calmed down, I rolled her back to her room and watched as an aide lifted her into bed, which appeared easier than it used to be. My mother weighed less now than even a few months ago.

When I visited the following day, I discovered that my mother was right. Someone *had* died.

• • •

It was Sue Ann, a wheelchair-bound nursing home resident with perfectly coiffed hair and tidy clothes who I always greeted and who always smiled broadly when I said hello. But I hadn't seen her in the TV lounge or dining room in a while.

After my usual visit with my mother the next day—during which she didn't mention a thing about the supposed death that had upset her so the night before—I rolled her into the dining room for lunch. I saw Mary, the resident who my mother had described as her "one real friend," sitting at a nearby table, and decided to ask her if she knew anything about Sue Ann.

"She passed away a few days ago," Mary said.

"I'm so sorry to hear that," I said.

"Listen, Mark," she said, touching my arm as her face grew serious. "I feel so bad for your mother. I always say hello to her, always try to talk to her. But sometimes she just sits there at the dining room table and cries."

I didn't even know how to respond to that. I summoned up a courteous response about how much I appreciated Mary's attentiveness and friendliness.

As the sliding glass doors in the lobby shushed open, I felt the urgent need to sit down. My mind couldn't handle walking any farther as I exited the building. I lowered myself on a bench just outside the doors. Usually, if I was feeling emotionally exhausted after my visit, I'd wait until I got home and collapse on the couch. In public, someone I knew might see me, and I'd feel compelled to put on a brave face and act like everything was fine.

Why do some people get to die while others have to keep living, even when they don't want to anymore?

Maybe Sue Ann was lucky. She got out. My mother had been ready and willing to depart for years. Yet there she was, trapped in a wheelchair, crying at the dinner table.

. . .

My mother stopped trying to memorize names and figure out where she was. She had become more focused on the basics, like determining when she should eat and when she had to go to the bathroom.

"How will they know to come get me?" she asked me one day. "What if they can't find me?"

"Don't worry, Momma, there's always someone here who knows exactly where you are. And you know what else? I always know exactly where to find you too. Every time I visit, I always find you right away. You've never heard me say that I had to look for you, right? You're always right where you need to be."

Eventually, she stopped being aware of when she needed to go the bathroom. The staff declared her incontinent. The nurses outfitted her with a catheter for a few weeks but explained that it was uncomfortable and shouldn't be a permanent solution. So they started putting diapers on her. At set times, nurse's aides showed up to hoist her into the bed to change her.

I could still wheel her around the facility, or even outdoors, as much as I wanted, but our array of activities shrank. Chilly autumn temperatures brought lovely colors to the trees outside of the nursing home windows, but they also meant it was too cold to roll around the block, or for us to go to the Mexican pizzeria nearby. So we stayed inside, touring the second and eighth floors, eating pizza in the sunroom or the library, and sitting in the lobby so we could people watch and gaze at the glistening koi fish in the giant fountain.

We still found things to talk about. Generally, the older the topic, the more my mother had to say. She told me about an early vacation she took with my father, right after World War II, at the Shore Meade Hotel in Miami Beach. We talked about her childhood friends in Louisville and the games they used to play in the street.

One day we were talking about a girl she used to play with back in Kentucky.

"I always had a lot of fun with Emmy—well, no, that's not right," she stopped and looked off into the distance, frowning. That name came from a different part of her past, but she couldn't recall the details. "That wasn't my friend's name. So who is Emmy?"

"Emmy was your granddaughter," I said. "She passed away, less than two years ago."

"How did she die?"

"She had a problem with her brain," I said. I didn't want to remind her about my niece's suicide because it had been very hard for her to deal with. "She was only thirty when she died."

My mother's brow tightened. "I *must* have known about that. But I really don't remember anything about it."

"It's okay. You did know about it, but it's been a while and you just forgot, that's all."

"Did she have kids?"

"No, she was single."

She looked down into her lap and sighed. "I really don't remember any of this. That's so sad."

"It's okay, Momma." I took her hand.

"Well, I guess in a way it's better that I didn't remember. It's very sad, but since it's already happened, there's nothing we can do about it."

• • •

Just after Thanksgiving, a lovely fake Christmas tree sprouted up next to the lovely fake fireplace in the Venerable Hills lobby. Candy cane decorations popped up on the wall behind the second-floor nurse's station. Holiday-themed music dominated the weekly live entertainment schedule. And greeting cards began piling up once again on my mother's bed—almost as many as she'd received for her ninetieth birthday the month before.

I opened each missive and read it to her before taping it to the wall above her bed.

"Look at all those cards, Momma!" I'd say, pointing to the array of greetings on the wall. "You have so many friends who are thinking about you."

"That's nice of people to think of me ... that really is a lot of cards." And she'd look away.

On Christmas Eve, Angel and I visited the nursing home with some friends. Angel brought Santa hats for us all to wear for the required selfie that we always took with my mother whenever we had a group visit.

The following day, Angel and I left on a long-planned trip to Mexico City. It was our first real vacation since my mother had moved to New York City. Even before leaving, I felt anxiety and guilt, like I was abandoning my mother. But Glynn had encouraged me to get away for a few days, and I actually had some assignments to work on in Mexico City. We organized carefully so that my mother wouldn't go long without visitors. Glynn would visit both weekends that I'd be gone, and her Brooklyn-based son would also stop by, as well as our friend Richard, who lived just a couple blocks away. As guilty as I felt, I agreed that spending some time away would probably be good for me.

• • •

Mexico City is especially festive during the Christmas season. A gigantic tree is placed in the Zócalo, one of the world's largest city squares. Multicolored lights grace the centuries-old buildings that line the streets of the historic downtown. Families stroll, hand in hand and arm in arm, as they bask in the holiday cheer.

I still thought about my mother every day while I was gone, but not every minute. I felt less tired. I was able to distract myself with sightseeing, sampling new foods, exploring museums, and going out at night. Angel encouraged me to live in the moment, and he knew how to make me smile with his cheerful disposition.

After arriving back in New York City, I felt like that Mexico City breather hadn't been worth it. The rush of emotions overwhelmed me more than if I'd simply stayed put, like a sudden wave rather than a constant flow, or if I'd delayed making payments on a loan and now had to double up to make up for lost time.

The first morning back, I walked through the TV lounge and saw my mother sitting there like always. But she was more frail, shrunken into her wheelchair. She was too weak to even blurt her usual "oh thank god" when she saw me.

"I really need to poop," she said instead.

Based on the smell, it seemed to me like she'd already gotten a head start on the pooping. I advised a nurse that my mother needed help as I rolled her to the library to chat and wait.

More than forty-five minutes passed. I walked over to the nurse's station, where the head nurse assured me that an aide would show up soon. I rolled my mother into her room for a change of scenery, and we talked about my Mexico City trip and her childhood. After nearly two hours had passed, Beatrice, the perennially unhappy aide, ambled into the room. She began throwing large paper sheets on the bed, creating the setting for a diaper change.

"I'm so glad you're here, Beatrice," I said. "We've been waiting a long time and my mother really has to use the toilet. I think she's already started."

Beatrice looked at us both and rolled her eyes. "Your mother doesn't have to go to the bathroom."

I lost it.

"Please don't roll your eyes at me, Beatrice," I said. "Don't give me a look like I'm being a jerk. You know I'm *always* nice to you, and I'm very frustrated because we've had to wait nearly two hours." Tears welled up in my eyes. Beatrice said nothing and walked into the bright yellow bathroom.

I followed her. "You know, it's really hard to come back home and see that she's even worse now than she was before," I said, my voice crackling.

Beatrice looked at my tears. "Don't cry," she said firmly. "Well, I can't *tell* you not to cry, but you have to be strong. My husband died last year, and I had to watch him get sicker and sicker. There's nothing you can do. You have to be strong for your mother."

I sighed and looked away. "You're right," I said. I went out to the library and waited for Beatrice to finish cleaning and changing my mother.

It seemed like I'd finally bonded with Beatrice. She'd shared something about her personal life for the first time. Maybe she really was trying to help. Maybe she wouldn't be rude to my mother anymore.

After about fifteen minutes, Beatrice opened the door. She stood there with one hand on her hip and the other holding my mother's slightly stained diaper straight into the air, like Lauren Bacall holding the bloody dagger in *Murder on the Orient Express*.

"Come here," she said. "You see? A little stain. But there was no bowel movement." I decided there was no use arguing.

The following day, however, Beatrice did something that for her was out of the ordinary: she made a helpful suggestion. She recommended that I buy a spill-proof sippy cup. "That way I can give it to your mother at bedtime and she can keep it with her in bed." I went out and bought one immediately.

33. Dual Citizenship

One day when I was about seven years old, I was rifling through my grandparents' dresser drawers. I wasn't trying to be nosey; I was just bored and I knew that Pop and Gran probably had drawing and painting materials stashed away somewhere. But something else caught my eye: a tiny pencil, stuck in between a stack of yellow-lined notepads that Pop used for drawing as well as to write his weekly Sunday school lessons.

The pencil wouldn't be any good for drawing, though. It measured only about three inches and was so thin that it would be lost in a pencil sharpener. Instead of being topped with an eraser, its blunt end was capped with the small plastic head of a very Black man, his eyes painted startlingly white with no pupils. Even stranger was the pencil holder: a minuscule plastic alligator. As I picked up both items, I realized that I was supposed to slide the pencil into the animal's mouth, so that only the man's head was visible. It looked like the creature was eating him alive.

"You shouldn't show that to anyone," my mother said when I brought it to her. "Just put it back where you found it."

This was the first time I'd found anything representing Black people in my grandparents' house. I knew the pencil was bad, but I didn't fully understand that this innocuous little doodad was designed to elicit chuckles from white people who might find it hilarious to see a Black person devoured by a wild animal. I found it curious—but also didn't understand why it couldn't have been a white person's head stuck into an alligator's mouth. I hid the pencil in my suitcase and took it home, where it found a permanent hiding place at the bottom of my sock drawer. As I got older, I was repulsed by the strange object, but I didn't know what to do with it. I didn't want to throw it out and have it land into the wrong hands. I felt this type of vicious humor needed to be documented and preserved, like a museum piece or something I could show my Northern friends who didn't understand the complex world I came from.

It's no wonder I was nervous about introducing my boyfriend to my Southern relatives.

• • •

Introducing your boyfriend to your family can be nerve-racking enough. Even more so if you're gay. And when your boyfriend is Puerto Rican and your relatives are Southern whites with very limited exposure to anyone outside of their own race and ethnicity, well, you can imagine why I felt the urge to crap my pants as Angel and I pulled into the driveway of my Uncle Ed and Aunt Agnes's vaguely Mediterranean-style tract home in the sun-soaked town of Bonita Springs, Florida.

Angel and I had been together for about two years when we decided to pay them a visit. I was twenty-eight and he was twenty-nine when we arranged a vacation in Miami Beach, which in the early 1990s was still lined with old folks sitting on lawn chairs in front of gloriously faded Art Deco masterpieces. It was a hip, offbeat destination with a vibrant gay nightlife, not yet polished or spoiled by the throngs of mainstream tourists and partiers who'd later descend on its renovated shores.

Less than three hours away, near the western end of a highway with the menacing name of Alligator Alley, sits

Bonita Springs, a small city on Florida's Gulf Coast where Ed and Agnes had built a beautifully spacious new home after retiring from their profitable careers in publishing and nursing in Louisville.

Of all my uncles and aunts, these were the only two who consistently made my life better in the years after my father died. Ever since I was four, they'd bought me clothes and toys. They gave me cash. They took my mother and me on trips to the big amusement parks in Florida and Virginia. They paid for half of my college education.

Ed and Agnes remained childless, generous, and wealthy. But they also happened to be less educated than my nuclear family (they entered the job market without college degrees) and, as far as I knew, had zero experience talking with anyone outside of their own racial and ethnic group. I had tapered off my visits to them over the years, partly because I got tired of their offensive comments about Black people.

• • •

It's not surprising that my uncle had racist views. He was born in 1911 in rural southeastern Kentucky. My father was born in the same place, just seven years later, but he developed very different views on race—aided, no doubt, by his education and life experience. Daddy was born in 1918, the youngest of ten kids in Baileys Switch, a Kentucky settlement that had grown around a camp occupied by Daniel Boone when he was laying out the Wilderness Road that early settlers used to move west. It wasn't exactly the most diverse place, even in the twentieth century.

My father got a bachelor's degree in English at Union College, a tiny United Methodist institution in Barbourville, just a few miles from his birthplace. After returning from World War II, he married my mother and moved them both to Atlanta so he could get a master's degree from Emory University, then started (but never completed) a PhD program at the University of Michigan in Ann Arbor. By the time he and my mother landed in Brockport, they'd both expanded their world view.

Ed, on the other hand, skipped college and stayed in the Bluegrass State. Other than his post-retirement move to Florida, he'd never lived farther from his birthplace than Louisville, where he launched a career in publishing at one of the city's biggest newspapers. It was kind of like the options presented in one of those board games designed to teach you about living; my father pointed his playing piece in the direction of college, and his brother headed straight for the money.

I'm not sure how much my father was exposed to people of other races during his early years, but I do know that he had Black friends and colleagues at the college where he later taught, in the small town in western New York where I was born. My mother said that he went out of his way, in fact, to rent our house to a Black family when we moved to Florida for a year (I was too young to notice what was going on, although one of the boys in that family later became a school friend of mine).

My mother was Southern, too, albeit from a much larger and more diverse city. Born in Louisville in 1925, I think she personally knew only one Black person—her family's cleaning woman—when she was growing up. Like most white people in the South in the early twentieth century, she didn't question segregation, although she later told me that as a child, she was troubled by the segregated water fountains. "I always thought it would be awful if you were a Black mother with a little child on a hot day and you couldn't even give him a drink of water," she said.

My mother later met people of various races, ethnicities, and nationalities as she moved around the eastern United States with my father. After he died, she completed her own bachelor's and master's degrees. She got involved in local politics and a variety of nonprofit organizations. She taught me about the importance of the Equal Rights Amendment when I was a kid in the 1970s, always noting that the Black civil rights movement was even more crucial. "Black people face even more challenges and prejudice than women do," she explained.

As far back as I can remember, my mother taught me that racism was wrong and that you shouldn't judge anyone based on their race, religion, or ethnicity. But she didn't teach me how to respond to prejudice directly. Southern manners dictate that you avoid conflict.

When you grow up with dual citizenship—Northern and Southern—you can sometimes find yourself in complicated situations, even with your own family.

• • •

What's ironic is that, from cuisine to music to religion, my relatives' lives benefited from the African American community and shared some of the same traditions, even as many Southern whites of that era limited their direct interaction with people of color.

My Uncle Ed and Aunt Agnes, for example, devoted countless hours avoiding places where Black people might be, feeling their livelihood threatened by Black people and bolstering their own insecurities by criticizing them.

It seemed that my extended family (but not my parents) purposely chose to live in neighborhoods that lacked diversity. When I was a teenager, I asked my grandmother why no Black people lived in Benton, their western Kentucky town. "There was one Negro family that lived here, many years ago," she said, using a term that was acceptable in her day. "But some neighbors drove them out of town. I believe they threw rocks at them. It was a shame how poorly that family was treated."

Decades later, I discovered that in 1908, Benton became what was called a "sundown town," a place that kept African Americans out by force or by local laws. The name comes from an unofficial policy that if Black people found themselves in those communities after the sun went down, they'd be shot, whipped, or killed. There were thousands of sundown towns around the country, and not just in the South.

None of my relatives lived in Benton in 1908, as far as I know—but some did live in nearby Birmingham, which drove its African American residents out that same year.

Some 300 miles east, something similar happened just one year after my father's birth in 1918, and just a few miles away from his home. A mob of white locals in the town of Corbin forced some 200 Black residents onto a freight train bound for Knoxville, forbidding them to return. Corbin was considered a sundown town from then on. In the 2010 census, its African American population was less than one percent.

My mother grew up in the larger, more sophisticated city of Louisville, but that metropolis had problems too. Whites living west of 30th Street—the West End neighborhood where my mother's family lived—changed the names of the streets to differentiate them from the adjacent Black neighborhoods. One month before my mother was born, in 1925, someone dynamited the home of an African-American family because they'd dared to buy property in a traditionally white area— just five blocks from my mother's childhood home.

A few weeks later, another Black family bought the house next door to that gentleman. Their home was dynamited too. Fortunately, the police offered protection, and the families were able to stay put.

I've never heard of any of my relatives being involved in any violent activity or confrontation with any African American. But I'm also pretty sure that none of them did anything to stop racist language or activity. And some of them—although not my parents—used racial slurs in conversations with other white people. My family was complicit.

• • •

Taking all this into consideration, you might forgive me for my over-the-top emotional reaction to what was likely a regular, everyday occurrence one evening when I was barely a teenager. My mother and I were spending the night at the Cordial Court Motor Inn near Columbus, Ohio. As was customary for me at that time, I went out for a walk after dinner in the retail complex behind the hotel (okay, I ventured out to stare at handsome anonymous traveling businessmen, but you've already heard about that).

The sky was dark as I walked through the parking lot back to the hotel. As I opened the glass door, I noticed an elderly couple getting out of a crimson sedan. They ambled slowly toward the door at the same glacial speed as my grandparents going to church. But this couple was African American. The man, outfitted in a stiff-looking formal suit and tie, was hunched slightly, like my grandmother. The woman's large, flowery dress distracted from her slender figure, and a small hat sat atop her perfectly coiffed hair. She was probably the same age as the man, but it looked like she could have walked faster if she hadn't been with him since she was standing straighter, patiently holding his arm and lovingly monitoring his every step.

My mother taught me to always hold doors for older people, so I smiled and stood there. And I kept standing there, for several minutes, with the door ajar, as they inched their way toward me. Up they finally went onto the curb. They smiled as they got closer.

"Thank you so much," the lady said, her eyes crinkling behind big glasses. "We're just moving a little slowly today."

"It's okay," I said, smiling back and pulling the door open a little more.

Finally, they got to the threshold. The ugly lights from the parking lot illuminated the man's deep wrinkles and warm smile.

"I knew I'd catch up with you someday," he said, nodding as he gently grasped the door frame and pulled himself through.

I froze briefly, the door handle still in my hand. I couldn't believe he'd just said that.

"Have a nice night!" I called as they continued down the hall.

Just before the trip, I'd watched *The Autobiography of Miss Jane Pittman*, a TV movie about an elderly African American lady who was born a slave in the 1800s and lived to see the civil rights movement in the 1960s. There was a final, dramatic scene in which—when she was more than one hundred years old—she finally got a chance to use what had always been a "Whites Only" water fountain. It reminded me of the fountains that my mother had told me about in Louisville when she was growing up, and how she'd felt bad that it might be hard for a mother to find a place for her child to get a drink of water.

I knew I'd catch up with you someday, the man had said to me.

Was it that significant that I'd held the door open for him? Was this the first time that a white person had extended this simple courtesy to him?

Tears formed in my eyes as I started walking back to my room.

I knew I'd catch up with you someday.

As I headed back to my hotel room, I thought some more. Maybe by "catching up," he was just making a pleasant joke about how long it took him to get to the door. I'd never know for sure. I wiped my tears and kept walking.

• • •

No matter what I write about racism in my family, something's going to come out wrong. How could I love my racist relatives? How could I have chosen to spend time with them? If I was such a progressive member of the liberal Northern branch of the family tree, why didn't I stand up more against their comments?

Well, I did what I could. Since no one taught me how to confront racism, it took me a while to learn. As a teenager, I watched more TV shows and movies about African American history and culture. But I still have trouble reconciling my love and appreciation of my relatives with the things they said.

My white friends from the New York City area, where I live now, often don't understand the concept of white guilt. Their parents and ancestors weren't in the United States when or where the worst atrocities occurred, so they don't have to wonder about what their relatives did or didn't do. But my family has been in the United States since the 1700s. There are always unanswered questions.

I started making changes to the family sing-alongs that we frequently did around the kitchen table. One of the songs we sang regularly was "Walking in the Parlor," which—some forty years later—I discovered was a nineteenth-century "Negro folk song" or "Negro minstrel song." I didn't know the origin of the work when I was a kid (nor did I know that such songs were often sung by white people in blackface). My grandparents and mother graciously accepted my edits to our family songbook, which mostly included my grandfather's favorite folk and pop music from the late nineteenth and early twentieth centuries.

My immediate family listened to my reasoning. With strangers it's not as likely. Here's an annoying thing about visiting the South when white: Some white people—people you don't even know—will assume that you're as racist as they are. Once, when I mentioned the name of the neighborhood where my mother grew up in Louisville to a local guy at a men's health club, he went off on a tangent about how Blacks had "ruined" that area.

"Well, I've driven through the West End recently, and the main difference I see is that they've planted more trees and gardens than there were when my mother lived there," I responded.

239

I also began countering my family's racist utterances. When Aunt Agnes told me to avoid a certain part of the beach near their house because Black people went there, I told her I didn't care who I shared the sand with. And when Uncle Ed warned me to always wipe off the top of soda pop cans because "Black people spit on them in the factories," I told him I was more worried about white people spitting. After each time I visited them as an adult, I took some of the money that they so generously gave me and donated it to the United Negro College Fund.

I doubted that I'd change anyone's way of thinking, but at least I wasn't silent anymore.

And now it was time for me to introduce Ed and Agnes to the love of my life. They didn't even know I was gay; that revelation would have to wait for another time. One step at a time. The first test: would they accept that I had a "friend" who wasn't white?

• • •

Honestly, I had faith that they would; otherwise, I wouldn't have suggested that we drive all the way to the Gulf Coast. My uncle and aunt were loving, generous people. And I was pretty sure that, when coming face to face with someone who wasn't white, they'd have the decency to be respectful.

As we nosed our polar white rental car into the driveway, Ed and Agnes ambled into the yard, beaming. It had been two or three years since I'd last visited, and they moved a bit slower now. They still looked the same, though. Uncle Ed still managed to hide most of his gray hair with ample applications of jet-black dye, and his ever-present paunch was encased in vibrant, high-rise plaid pants that would have been perfect on a 1970s golf course. Aunt Agnes was stiffly erect in her posture, walking as if she had a wooden leg. They hugged me and—more importantly—they hugged Angel. We were off to a good start.

They took us to get barbecue for dinner, one of our traditional family favorites. Strangely, Ed ordered one dish for Angel and me to share. Was that a nod to the fact that we were a couple? Not likely. I think he just knew that the servings were too big for one person. As we dug into sloppy servings of ribs, corn on the cob, and cornbread, Angel and I told them about our vacation in Miami Beach and our jobs in New York City, and they regaled Angel with stories about how amazingly cute I was as a little boy. It was as good a conversation as I could have hoped for.

After dinner, we went back to their house and settled into the family room for a supermarket-bought pecan pie that Aunt Agnes whisked out of the refrigerator. Uncle Ed pulled the lever to raise the footrest on his plush recliner.

Then the conversation got weird.

"There are a lot of HipSpanish in Florida," Uncle Ed told Angel, who nodded politely. I attempted to control my grimace as Ed went on to explain how the "HipSpanish" (as he apparently thought "Hispanic" was pronounced) were much better people to have around than "the Blacks." In Miami, he said, the Blacks were always stealing ten-speed bicycles. He knew it was true because he'd seen it on the news.

"Oh, I didn't know that," Angel responded diplomatically. Like me, he wanted to make a good impression. And like me, he knew that there wasn't much you could do when talking to someone like my uncle.

Perhaps out of desperation for the evening to end, Angel finished his entire dessert rather quickly.

"JEE-ZUS WANTS SOME MORE PECAN PIE!" Ed suddenly called out, turning to Agnes.

Angel smiled politely and looked at me, raising his eyebrows slightly—I assumed he was as confused about being called Jesus as I was. Agnes darted up as if it were a fire drill, grabbing Angel's empty plate from his hands and scurrying into the kitchen to fetch another slice. I followed her.

"What. Is. His. Name?" she whispered with strained emphasis on every word, her face beet red beneath the bright fluorescent lighting as she sliced into the pie.

"It's Angel," I deadpanned.

She pursed her lips and shook her head like it was about to explode. "I *told* Ed his name wasn't Jee-zus! That was the name of the Mexican who used to work in our yard!"

"Ohhhh, okay." I took the plate from her and returned to the family room, where Ed was continuing his scholarly discourse. I'd warned Angel about the possibility of idiocy and racism during our visit. We both knew we'd never change their way of thinking. Ed remained oblivious that his topic of conversation was offensive. Maybe Agnes did have an inkling, and that's why her face looked even more like Gary Sinise sniffing glue.

Later that evening, Angel and I talked quietly in the guest room where he was to sleep (Ed and Agnes didn't know we were gay, so we were assigned separate bedrooms. One step at a time).

"I'm so sorry about the conversation tonight and the ten-speed bicycle comment and all that shit," I said. "They're so racist. I sometimes call them out about it, but I just don't know what to do. This is so embarrassing."

"Well yeah, the stuff they said was racist," Angel said. "But they're old, they're from Kentucky, and you'd already told me they're not very smart. I'm not going to argue with them. My own aunt in Puerto Rico has said stupid and racist things. But I love her and she's been good to me, so I have to accept that she is the way she is. We just laugh about it. Uncle Ed and Aunt Agnes have been good to you too. And they're trying to be nice to me. But some people just aren't going to change."

"And I'm sorry he was calling you Jee-zus."

"It's okay." He smiled. "I didn't even think that was racist. I just thought it was stupid."

34. Flushing Out the Truth

New York City, January 2016

Why do the most pressing phone calls always come when you're trying to sleep? One morning just before the sun rose, my cell started clanging just as I dreamed about missing a flight connection in some random airport.

"Your mother has fallen," the nurse said. "We think she was reaching for something on the floor during breakfast, but she lost her balance and hit her head on the table as she fell. She seems to be okay now, but she bled quite a bit. We need to know if you'd like her to go to the emergency room, just to make sure that she's all right."

What was I going to say, no?

I didn't have time to shower. I threw on a pair of old, ripped jeans and the T-shirt I'd been planning to wear to the gym and rushed over.

A bloody bandage covered my mother's forehead. She was sitting up in bed, straighter than usual, smiling and perky. She somehow seemed more alert, more energetic.

I gave her the customary hug and kiss hello.

"Tell me what happened, Momma!"

"Well, I don't know." She was still smiling, as if we were joking about having lost her car keys.

"Did you fall?"

"I don't remember falling."

"Can you feel that bandage on your forehead? The nurse said she thinks you were reaching for something on the floor in the dining room, and then you fell and bumped your head on the table."

She touched the bandage and smiled again. "Well, if that's the case, I hope I was reaching for something good, so it was worth the fall!"

Medics appeared a few minutes later and bundled my mother onto a stretcher for our ambulance ride to a nearby medical center. We spent most of the day waiting in a bustling emergency room filled with distant conversations, high-tech beeps, and clanging metal. Every now and then, a white-garbed staff member would appear to ask questions, take a reading of my mother's vital signs, and then disappear. I sat down next to her wheeled bed, rested my head on the safety bar, and briefly fell asleep. She seemed to stay awake because when I opened my eyes again, she was still sitting up, calmly observing the nonstop activity around us.

Finally, an aide grabbed the bed and rolled my mother into an examination room to investigate the injury. By now, her forehead sported a sizeable bump. After the scan, they shuffled us back to the emergency room to await the results.

Nearly an hour later, a long-faced doctor in a long lab coat appeared.

"Would you mind stepping away to give me a few minutes to speak with your mother?" he asked.

He closed the curtains around her bed as I walked away.

After a few minutes, the doctor emerged. "Could you come with me?" He asked. "I'd like to find a place where we can speak privately."

I followed him into the hall, where he pulled over a chair and asked me to sit down.

"I needed to speak with your mother first, to ask her permission to talk to you about this. The test came back." He paused. "It shows that your mother has a rather sizeable tumor."

I stared blankly. "Oh ... well ... is this something different from the tumor that they found in July?"

The doctor's eyebrows raised. "She has already received this diagnosis?"

"Yes, we already knew about the tumor. And my mother didn't want any treatment for it. She was mentally aware when the diagnosis was made, and she said she's too old to undergo treatment."

"Oh. Well," he shifted in his seat and adjusted his collar. "We didn't receive any records from the nursing home, so we didn't know. We'll continue to review the results of the most recent tests to see if there's anything new."

I walked back to the curtained area where my mother was lying. She smiled.

"What did the doctor say to you?" she asked as I took her hand.

"What did he tell *you*?" I asked, not wanting to remind her unnecessarily about her condition. She hadn't mentioned the tumor a single time since arriving in New York City. She'd most likely forgotten about it, and I didn't see a reason to remind her if she didn't remember what the doctor had just told her today.

"He said they found a brain tumor."

"That's what he told me too," I said, "but you know that's something that we found out about last year, so there's nothing new that we have to worry about."

"Well," my mother paused and squeezed my hand. "If the brain tumor does me in that's okay because I've had a very long and happy life."

• • •

My mother's calmness reminded me of when she first shared the bad news by phone from a hospital bed in Rochester. She was very composed then, too, and more aware of her situation. The drama was all on my end.

245

"Well, sweetie, they tell me I have a brain tumor," she had said.

"Oh, no ... Momma." I paused. I breathed. "So what do we do? What did the doctors say they can do?"

In a voice that was frail yet determined, she explained that she'd already lived a good life and was too old to put herself through any excruciating treatment. "When it's time to go, it's time to go, kiddo."

"But are you in pain?"

"Nothing hurts. I'm just tired, but they've got me well drugged. But I ..." she swallowed and her voice wavered, "... sometimes I don't know where I am or what I'm supposed to be doing. Sometimes I just feel *lost*." She paused again and regained her earlier tone. "Your old momma is crazy, kid."

I told her not to worry about a thing. I told her we'd do everything we could to make sure she's comfortable. I told her that Glynn and I would visit her again soon and figure out everything. I told her I loved her.

And then I hung up.

Tears clouded my vision as I dropped to the floor of my bedroom. I stared at the side of the bed but all I could see was my mother's face, her hands.

I jumped up and rushed to the bookcase, pulling out a box that overflowed with old family photos. I rifled through the oily snapshots as urgently as if I were a game show contestant. I needed to see photos of us together.

I found a black-and-white snapshot of my mother, wearing a tiny pillbox hat and holding the infant version of me, back when she said I looked like Winston Churchill. I threw the photo on the bed. Next, I pulled out the only portrait I've ever seen of our entire nuclear family (my father was usually behind the camera). That photo landed on the bed too.

I found a few more to add to the pile: a pastel-hued snapshot of my mother and a nine-year-old me, smiling in a hotel pool beneath the Florida sunshine. A flyer with a headshot from one of my mother's unsuccessful political campaigns. A portrait I took of her in the front yard when she was in her seventies. And a photo from our last trip to California to visit her sister, when they were both in their eighties. The three of us were standing, smiling bravely in front of the assisted living facility where my aunt lived.

"If I ever get to the point where I have go into a nursing home, just shoot me," my mother told me right after that visit.

I kept digging for photos. Something white in the depths of the box caught my eye. But it wasn't a photo. It was a long-forgotten envelope from Pop, my grandfather. Inside was a fresh dollar bill and a letter dated 1973, in which he tried to comfort me after our dog, Garçon II, had died.

I want you to grow up and be self-sufficient and independent and be able to meet and overcome the rough spots in life that everybody must have, he had typed. *Your conversation on the phone Sunday, in regard to the loss of Gar #2, saddened us, but we saw that you were a manly little fellow in your thinking, and reasoning things out. We know that the things that happen in this life that we can't do anything about, we are not to grieve over too much.*

It was like some magical coincidence that I had pulled out words of wisdom from my grandfather at a time like this.

I wiped my eyes and put the box back on the bookshelf. I grabbed a plastic envelope and placed Pop's letter and the photos from the bed inside, and then placed it on my desk. I'd need to refer to it again soon.

35. Eunice's Tips for Traveling with an Elderly Parent

(when you're not inside an ambulance, obviously—
we came up with these tips for my travel blog,
LatinFlyer.com, after years of traveling to California
together when she was in her eighties)

1. Reserve an accessible hotel room. Even if your parent isn't physically disabled, an accessible room has more safety features, like additional railings in the bathroom. Renting a four-door car is also usually a good idea; they're often easier to get in and out of.
2. Plan extra connecting time for air travel. When making airline reservations, allow more time than you'd usually need to make connections. Also remember, you may be the first ones to board the plane, but you'll be the last ones off.
3. Bring lots of small bills. If you're using a wheelchair service in the airport for arrivals, departures and connections, you should tip the hard-working people who shuttle passengers around.
4. Ask the valet to leave the wheelchair at the gate. Try to keep the wheelchair until boarding. You never know when there may be a last-minute gate change, or when your parent may need to go to a far-off bathroom.

5. This tip came from a helpful flight attendant: If you need a wheelchair when you land, *do not get off the plane* until you see the wheelchair at the gate. If you deplane and the wheelchair is late, you may be waiting without a place to sit on the jetway or at the arrival gate. The aircraft in which you've just arrived cannot start boarding for its next leg until you've gotten out. So if you wait on board, the crew will have to speed up the arrival of a wheelchair.

36. The Layover

Dallas/Fort Worth International Airport, 2016

When it opened in 2005, the people mover that connects terminals at Dallas/Fort Worth International Airport was the world's largest system of its kind. Its sparkling cars zip along at speeds of up to thirty-five miles an hour, transferring passengers efficiently among the airport's five semi-circular terminal buildings.

Luckily, I had more connecting time than usual while waiting to transfer between terminals on the afternoon of March 7, when my cell phone rang.

"Your mother has stopped eating and drinking," the head nurse said solemnly. "She's dehydrated and weak, and we've had to keep her in bed. We're going to connect her to an IV to provide hydration. But it's not looking good. It would be a good idea to visit as soon as you can. I don't know if she can make it for very long."

There's not much to say when you get a call like that, especially when you're standing in an airport more than a thousand miles away. I explained that I was en route back to New York City and that it would be quite late by the time I landed, but that I'd visit the first thing in the morning or late that night if they felt it was necessary enough to warrant overriding the nursing home's strict visiting hours. She said we could wait until the morning, but that she'd call me if anything changed.

I'd already felt bad about being away from my mother, but a big tour operator and vacation packager had hired me for a high-paying, career-defining consulting gig that required me to spend nearly two weeks in Colombia, helping them to research and create new tour packages. On the way home, I'd stopped for a quick visit in Panama to see friends and decompress. Now, reality had slapped me in the face before I'd even boarded my connecting flight.

. . .

You know how it is when you're having problems with your boyfriend or girlfriend and every song on the radio seems to apply to your situation? The same can happen, apparently, when your mother is wasting away in a nursing home. Every time I turned on the TV music channel in the Bogota apartment where I stayed, the song "Stressed Out" by twenty one pilots was playing. The songs "Middle" by DJ Snake and Bipolar Sunshine and "7 Years" by Lukas Graham, meanwhile, made me tear up.

I'd barely mentioned my mother's situation to anyone in Colombia, but she was always on my mind. I saw her face in the warm eyes and plump cheeks of our tour guide, whose ready smile seemed lifted directly from a photo of my mother standing next to her maroon four-door sedan in Florida, circa 1968.

I'd explained to my mother that I wouldn't be away for long. And I'd made sure she wouldn't be alone. My sister stopped by every weekend, and Angel and our friend Richard both visited regularly while I was gone. They texted me selfies with her, and she was always smiling. Everything would be fine. I still felt guilty.

. . .

Now, as I wandered the concourse at Dallas/Fort Worth, the next chapter was unfolding. I still had a couple of hours to kill, and the chilly airport made me realize I'd been stupid to pack my winter coat in my checked baggage. My nose started running, and I began sneezing. I'd arranged a gangly trip home using frequent flyer miles that included two layovers, so this was going to be a long day. I stopped for my favorite DFW layover meal: Texas barbecue. But the pulled pork lacked its usual tang.

I was exhausted by the time I boarded the American Eagle flight from Dallas/Fort Worth to Memphis. I tried to sleep, but it was impossible. I pulled out a pen and lowered the tray table. A eulogy for my mother poured onto the paper in front of me. I wrote it to her many friends, who I imagined would attend the memorial service, whenever that might be, if we held it in Brockport.

My mother loved Brockport. And she loved all of you, too.

I wrote about how she came to love her adopted hometown of Brockport, even though she first thought she wouldn't like small-town life. I wrote about how she made so many good friends. A lot of those friends—the ones who were still living—would be sitting in front of me, I imagined.

I wrote about how she loved her part-time job at the historical society so much that she didn't retire until age eighty-eight. To lighten things up, I mentioned how she told me in recent years about a guy she dated before getting married, a good-looking young man she'd met before my father. He was a really good kisser, she said. But she broke it off with him after he mailed her a letter riddled with grammatical errors and misspellings. Even as a teenager, she was exacting when it came to words.

I wrote about the time she scared off the pesky Southern Baptist minister during my grandfather's calling hours. And how once, when she had to go to the emergency room in

Brockport years earlier, the staff had to ask my mother and her friends to quiet down because they were laughing and talking so much.

I wrote about her involvement with the history club, the church, Amnesty International, and the hospital's fund-raising organization. And how she ran for office twice and lost twice. And how she managed to get undergraduate and graduate degrees, even while working and raising me single-handedly.

I asked her once, in more recent years, how she could possibly have managed to raise a bratty kid, get her college degrees, work, and do all the other things she did back then.

"You just do what you have to do," was her simple answer.

Since the connecting flight from Memphis to New York City had only five passengers on board, the gate agent said we could all board early and sit in first class. I didn't hear anything new from Venerable Hills, so I collapsed into bed when I finally made it home, long after midnight.

37. The Snow Globe

New York City, March 8-11, 2016

My mother was a different person when I arrived the next morning. She was lying in bed, her head tilted to one side at an odd, uncomfortable-looking angle, as if she'd fallen asleep unexpectedly. But she was awake. She stared blankly toward one corner of the room, her lids half-closed. Her body seemed thinner than the last time I'd seen her, just twelve days earlier. An IV tube pierced one arm and the low-cut hospital gown hung lower than before, revealing the box-like outline of the pacemaker that had been placed in her chest several years earlier.

I walked to the side of the bed where she could see me. She smiled when she saw me but didn't move her head. I kissed her cheek and held her hand.

"How are feeling, Momma? Have you eaten anything?" I asked.

"I'm too nauseated to eat," she said slowly. "I'm afraid I'd just throw it up."

She was the same the next day. And the next.

The cold I'd caught on the trip gripped me, exacerbated by the stress of seeing my mother in such bad shape. I spent three consecutive daily visits sitting next to her on the bed, my face covered with a paper surgical mask so I wouldn't get her sick. I held her hand and gazed at a drawing on the wall that my nephew had made of her just one month earlier. In the illustration, she was smiling and sitting at a table in her wheelchair, sketching with a colored pencil. My eyes welled with tears.

On the third day, she turned to me.

"It's nice that we have these few extra days with you and Angel," she said. "And then if this part of our life ends, at least we know we've had a nice time."

Tina, the head nurse, advised me that it wasn't healthy for my mother to be lying down all day because it increased the risk of pneumonia. Before one of my daily visits, the staff tried placing her in a new, high-backed wheelchair—the kind they used with patients who basically couldn't move on their own. But my own mother was too weak to sit, even in that chair. They put her back to bed and reattached the IV before I returned later in the day.

I was no longer tempted to steal bites from the meals they served in the nursing home; they now arrived in pureed form, everything a nearly identical consistency. I arranged my visits to be there for lunch or dinner, so I could feed her and encourage her to eat. But even after four days of taking medication to combat nausea, she still turned away from me after eating just a bite or two.

"Do you still feel nauseated?" I asked after she refused a spoonful of mashed potatoes.

"No."

"If you're not feeling nausea anymore, what makes you not want to eat?" I asked.

She sighed. "Because I've *just had it*. I've had a good life, and I'm ready to go."

The next day, Tina walked into the room and asked if I would step into the hall.

"I think it would be a good time to consider enrolling your mother in hospice care," she said. "That will provide an additional layer of care, on top of what we are already giving her."

I started crying.

"You've been a good son," Tina said. "Not many kids would do what you've done. You've got to be strong."

"I know, I know." I swallowed. "Can you tell me how long my mother might last? I mean, I know you can't really predict something like that, but just a ballpark estimate?"

"It's impossible to say. But I would guess weeks, not months."

That night, I dreamed that I visited my mother as she lay in a wintery, snow-covered field that glistened blue-white in the moonlight. She was asleep in a clearly artificial snow-bank with light, sparkly flakes of snow like you'd see in a fantasy movie about a princess or in one of those snow globes I had when I was a kid. I kneeled next to her, slowly covering her body with the fluffy flakes. Then I put a clear glass pane over her face before starting to pile the snow over her face. Like Sleeping Beauty.

38. A Different Journey

"How are you feeling?" the voice on the phone asked me. "How are you dealing personally with the situation?"

It was the first time that anyone other than my husband or a couple of friends had asked me how *I* was doing. Tears welled up in my eyes.

The call came from a counselor at a hospice care organization. The kind-sounding man, Tom, explained how the hospice service would work, including the visitation schedule and what the hospice nurse could and couldn't do. Essentially, the nurse's goal would be to make my mother as comfortable as possible and to help me with any medical decisions or questions if need be.

"You're going through a lot," Tom said. Those few words of acknowledgement comforted me. "Do you have a support system—people you can talk to and who can help?"

"Yes, more than anyone it's my husband. If it weren't for him, I probably would need to be in psychotherapy by now."

"That's very good. We also have support services for family members, and since your mother is now enrolled with us, you're eligible for that as well."

For some reason, I had always assumed that hospice care involved moving someone to a special, dedicated facility with solemn-faced staff, complicated-looking beds, and strange equipment in every corner. Perhaps it would be set in a Victorian-era mansion, with a rolling lawn and heavily starched nurses.

But in my mother's case, placing her into this type of care meant she'd stay put in the nursing home and that a hospice nurse would visit her on a near-daily basis, to complement the service and support offered by the Venerable Hills staff.

Tom explained that hospice workers have a different approach compared to nursing home staff and other medical professionals. "People who work at nursing homes are basically trained to *respond* to medical situations," he said. "They're programmed to respond and treat, with the goal of keeping patients alive. Hospice care is designed to evaluate options to help family members make decisions and to provide support and care, rather than just responding and treating without considering alternatives. So if you have any questions about anything that might happen moving forward, you can talk to the visiting nurse assigned to this case, or you can call our help line, or you can call me directly."

• • •

The next day, I sat at a table in the nursing home library with Antonio, the main nurse assigned to my mother's hospice care. He was in his early thirties, his scrubs snug around the amount of extra weight that you might expect on someone who has a stressful job trying to help people at the end of their lives.

"How are you holding up?" he asked me with a calm, focused gaze.

"I'm okay," I said. Tears filled my eyes yet again. I guess since so few people had asked me how I felt, the questions from the hospice people uncovered more of my own emotions. My mother was lying in her room, just a few feet away. At first, I feared she'd hear us, but I realized she wouldn't be able to.

"It's just hard ... seeing her like this," I said. "We visit her as often as possible and we help her eat and drink when she wants to, and we hold her hand. I don't know what else to do."

"That's good," he responded. His tone was soothing but serious. I think he looked at me the whole time but I'm not sure because I kept looking at the floor and the empty chair beside me.

"Physical contact is very important," he continued. "It's also important to realize that, even if it seems like she's sleeping or not conscious—or if she has difficulty talking or expressing herself—that doesn't mean she can't hear and understand what we're saying. So always keep talking to her."

"Okay, we will."

"Another thing to keep in mind: Sometimes people hold on because they're worried about family members. You can make her feel better by assuring her that you and the rest of your family are okay and that you're going to be okay, no matter what."

"All right," I said. I swallowed and stared at the table. "How long do you think she might live?"

"I'd say about a month. Your mother is on a different journey now."

39. Maybe We Should Have Had Kids

New York City, March 2016

I'm losing my mind.

The lockers at the gym were glossy blue, like if you shellacked a robin's egg. Ventilation holes punctuated their sleek façades. Some lockers were cinched closed with locks. Some were ajar. But they all looked the same.

The high-energy pop music pulsing through the air was designed to keep people moving. But now, I was completely still, staring at the lockers. Confused.

I couldn't remember where I'd left my street clothes.

Exercising a few times a week made me feel better and, I assumed, helped to relieve some of the stress of worrying about my mother. As the brain tumor diminished her ability to remember and accelerated my anxiety, the comforting routine of lifting weights gave me some sense of control.

But now I'd lost control.

Since these were unassigned lockers, I tried to always choose one in the same area, on the wall farthest from the bathroom. After today's workout, I had strutted confidently toward a lock that looked like mine and thrust my key toward it. But the key didn't fit.

I scanned the entire row. I looked at the lockers below. I didn't see any other locks like mine.

I stepped back and stood there for a minute.

No big deal, right? It's got to be here. But wait. What if someone stole my stuff and that's why I can't find it? What if I'd accidentally left the lock open?

It didn't seem that would be likely. At any rate, I'd need to tell the guy at the front desk which locker was mine before he'd take my claim seriously. But I didn't know which one I'd used.

What am I going to do if I never find my locker? It's already happening. I'm starting to lose my memory, lose my ability to function. This must run in the family. I could have a brain tumor like my mother right now, without even knowing it. Or I could have the beginnings of dementia, like my aunt.

It's almost time for me to visit Momma again. She knows who I am, but she can't even remember if she's had breakfast this morning. And here I am, standing around like an idiot. Lost in the locker room.

Some of the guys standing near me were dressing. Some were undressing. Some were chatting, in English and Spanish and another language I couldn't identify. One guy smelled like he should have applied more deodorant.

This can't be happening.

I was embarrassed. I was afraid that people could tell that I was lost. I sat down on a bright red metal bench and hunched over my cell phone as if that were what I really, absolutely needed to do at that very moment.

Some important text message from work. Yes. That's why I'm not opening my locker, that's what people will think now. I need to wait until the locker room empties out. I don't want other people to see me frantically searching every corner, trying to find a locker that has my lock on it. They might think I'm trying to steal things from other people. Or they might think I've gone crazy.

It was almost like my teenage days pretending to search for a lost bathing suit, as an excuse to spend more time in the locker room at the Cordial Court Motor Inn in Ohio. But now *I* was one of the older guys, and I didn't want to be looking for excuses to linger. I just wanted to find my locker.

Who's going to oversee my mother's well-being if I can't even remember where my own locker is? My sister lives two hours away. It will fall on poor Angel. He didn't plan on this when he married me.

How much time do I have until retirement, anyway? Sixteen, seventeen years, if I can stay healthy enough to work until age seventy and get maximum social security benefits. The years fly by so quickly. All the adults who were around when I was a kid are either dead or dying or have lost their minds. I'm next in line. I'm reaching the end of my active adult life. There probably won't be any more career shifts. No big new dreams. It's just a matter of time until I'm in the same shape as my mother. And it will probably come sooner rather than later.

And who the fuck is going to take care of me if I can't remember anything and I'm the one sitting in a nursing home? All I have is Angel, but he's the same age as me. We're basically alone, on our own, after more than twenty years together. I know you shouldn't have kids just because you want someone to take care of you when you're old, but maybe I should have pushed him for us to adopt.

Where is my fucking locker?

There was a lull in the flow of patrons. I was the only one in the room now. I jumped up and began my hunt, methodically inspecting every single locker, from one corner of the room to the next.

After about seven minutes, I found my belongings. They were tucked away in a far corner, where I'd never stored anything before.

I went home, changed, and walked to the nursing home, preparing to smile for my mother.

40. Counting Calories

New York City, March 2016

"Oh man, let me tell you—it took forever before Sylvester would eat anything other than plain crackers," my neighbor Greta said as she sipped a cocktail from a clear plastic cup. "If it weren't for those crackers, he would have starved to death."

We'd invited a few neighborhood friends over for drinks one wintery afternoon and, as their kids played in the living room, the parents were sharing childrearing stories in the kitchen. Veronica chimed in. "Tell me about it. My first kid would only eat cheese for nearly four months. We thought he was going to turn into a cow. Plus, it took him so long to toilet train, his room stank for months."

This conversation was charming and acceptable, not depressing and uncomfortable, because they were discussing their kids. You can talk about bizarre eating habits. You can talk about poop and puke. You can share war stories about the craziest, grossest, and most challenging situations—as long as the person you're talking about is a child.

But when it's your parent? Well, no. People don't want to hear about that.

We as humans can comfortably discuss people who are *developing* their facilities, but not those who are *losing* them.

I wanted to share my stories too.

But I didn't say a thing. I laughed politely.

"One thing you can't go wrong with is those little fish-shaped crackers," our neighbor Jack interjected after taking a swig of beer. "Mark and Angel, you guys are the best. Of all the people who we visit, you're the only ones who think to have stuff like that—things that the kids like."

"I love them too," I said, daring to venture further. "I take bags of them over to my mother at Venerable Hills. They're one of the few things she can easily eat by herself."

"Kudos, guys, you always know what to do."

The conversation continued about the children. There aren't usually follow-up questions about aging parents. I leaned back against the kitchen counter, smiling and watching their lips move.

...

I doubled my visits to daily until the visiting hospice nurse service started, skipping only a couple of days when exhaustion kept me on my own couch. I'd sometimes ask Angel to roll me a joint, which calmed me by blurring my thoughts, delivering me to a state not unlike that of my mother at times.

I also started canceling trips: No more Fort Lauderdale to see Angel's family (he went without me but cut his visit short). Forget about Puebla for Mexico's annual tourism conference. The travel bloggers' conference in Minnesota would have to make do without me. I also wouldn't be able to cover Mexico City's Pride celebration or make the annual trek to visit my best friend from high school in Chicago.

I needed to be close to my mother, and I couldn't bear the idea of leaving and coming back to find her in even worse shape or having her die when I wasn't there.

Like doting parents of a fussy toddler, Angel and I became laser-focused on food consumption—specifically, the kinds of food my mother would and wouldn't eat.

It wasn't like we hadn't been paying attention to my mother's culinary preferences before. She hadn't really been interested in eating since arriving in New York City. "The food is fine here," she once said as she pushed away a plate of half-eaten turkey. "It's just not anything I want to eat every day."

I sometimes ate her leftovers at Venerable Hills (travel writers like free food), and I agreed with her appraisal of the facility's cuisine. Nursing home food is like a lesser version of airline food: okay for one meal, but you wouldn't want to make it your daily diet. But my mother had no choice, except when I brought her food or took her out to the pizzeria across the street. Since arriving in New York City, her only favorites had been cola and potato chips, sometimes accompanied by a tasty dip that Angel made.

But those days were over. She didn't care about any food at all now. She was losing weight. The staff started bringing her little boxes of fruit-flavored nutritional drinks, which were packed with calories and vitamins. But she refused to drink them. "Yuck," she'd say after one sip. "That's way too sweet."

In the past, Angel and I avoided visiting during lunch and dinner hours (she used to eat in the dining room, where they didn't allow visitors during mealtime), but now we reworked our schedule to be present at mealtime so we could help her eat as she reclined in bed. But the food that arrived at her bedside failed to entice her.

"It's only natural that she doesn't want to eat anymore," my sister reasoned, with all the logic in the world. "Her body's shutting down."

Angel and I weren't trying to force-feed her. We just didn't want her to suffer from thirst or hunger simply because she was too weak to feed herself. We helped her when she needed it. By now, my mother never took more than three or four bites of food before turning her head and saying, "That's enough." Then we'd move the tray away.

Angel and I kept close track of what she ate. If one of us went alone to see her, we'd later share every minor detail about what she said, did, ate, and drank. Numbers figured heavily in our daily life now: how many spoonfuls of ice cream or soup did she consume? How many bites of egg salad or tuna sandwich did she accept? How many sips of water did she take?

Angel figured out a clever way to get her to drink the overly sweet nutritional beverage; he emptied the container into a cup with lots of ice and hid the box. His mother-in-law would often drink the whole thing, unaware that it was her least favorite beverage.

I always tried to estimate the number of calories that she'd ingested. But it was never much.

We excitedly recounted whenever she ate or drank more than usual and were thrilled when we found something new that she liked. Small crackers, for example, were easy; she could reach into the bag herself, although she wasn't always successful at actually putting the food in her mouth.

One afternoon, I was having an especially difficult time finding anything that caught her interest on the tray.

"I don't like the looks of that," she said when I'd offer her some mashed potatoes or meatloaf. She took a tiny sip of water from the flexible straw and then waved it away.

"No, sweetie, I don't want anything," she said. I felt helpless.

"I don't know what to do, Momma," I said. "What should I do for you?"

"Just hold my hand."

41. If I Forget

New York City, March 2016

We talked as much as I could keep a conversation going. I sang to her; mostly Broadway show tunes, which she seemed to like better than the big band and 1940s pop I played when she first moved to New York City. Music from *Chicago, Gypsy,* and *South Pacific* made her smile and tap her fingers.

And I still did the Quiz Show from time to time. Depending on how she was feeling, she usually still got most of the answers right.

"What's your full name?"

"Eunice Clayton Chesnut."

"What's my name?"

"Mark Edward Chesnut."

"What was your father's name?"

"Charles Dexter Clayton."

"When's your birthday?"

She was silent for a minute. "I'm not sure."

"November what?"

Then she'd get it right.

"And what are the names of your sister and brother?"

She looked at me. "I don't remember."

"Rarene and Don."

"Oh."

She paused and blinked, then looked at me again. "If I forget who you are, will you still remember me?"

42. What's-His-Name

New York City, March 2016

During the month of March, I was on the verge of tears nearly every day. I listened to the soothing voice of 1990s pop singer Seal on my cell to stay calm.

Sometimes I exited Venerable Hills so tired that I had to rest on a bench in front of the building or sit in the garden behind my apartment before going upstairs.

My mother, on the other hand, kept a positive attitude, even when she talked about death. She may have been bed-ridden and going downhill, but her sense of humor and sweetness compensated for her fading physical strength.

"I've had a very good life," she said slowly one day as she lay in her bed, propped up with pillows and sipping ice water through a flexible straw. "You've been a wonderful son, and we have a lot of happy memories of all the things we've done."

"You're right, Momma, we really have had a lot of good times."

Her brow furrowed. "But you know, I really wish I could just go to sleep and not wake up," she paused. "Although I really would like to see what's-his-name one more time."

"Who would you like to see?" I asked.

She looked at me and cocked her head. "Well, I don't know." She cracked a smile and burst out with a wonderful staccato cackle of a laugh. "I guess if I can't even remember who I'm talking about, then it doesn't really matter if I see him or not!"

. . .

Other times, her confusion unintentionally brought up heavy topics.

One afternoon as I fed her a spoonful of cheap vanilla ice cream (you don't get fancy desserts at a nursing home), she stopped eating and looked at me. She frowned in her way that I knew meant she was pondering something important.

"After we eat, do we die?"

The tumor was increasingly hindering her ability to find the right words. But I'd reached a point where I almost always knew what she meant, even if she couldn't articulate it. In this case, I assumed that she wanted to ask if she would *poop* after eating since she had recently become quite interested in discussing bowel movements and urination.

Still, I answered the question as she asked it.

"Well, I don't know if we'll die right after we eat, but you're free to do whatever you need to do when you feel the time is right."

"Okay," she said, taking a sip of water from the flexible straw that I held in front of her. "I think I've had about enough to eat for now."

She pushed away the tray and looked around her room, as if there might have been something new and interesting that she hadn't seen before.

She turned back to me. "I'm afraid."

"What are you afraid of?"

"Losing you," she answered, smiling and squeezing my hand. Honestly, I knew that was a bullshit answer. She was trying to be nice and had either forgotten her original thought or was trying to avoid being morbid.

"Well, don't worry about losing me. I'm fine and I'll be around for you, no matter what."

"Okay, I'm glad to hear that."

I was still curious about what she really feared, even though I could guess what it was. So I asked another question. "Are you afraid of dying?"

"No. I'm afraid of being here."

43. Oxygen

New York City, April 9-10, 2016

On Saturday, April 9, at about 9:30 p.m., a phone call interrupted the TV show that Angel and I were watching (don't ask me what the program was; my memory is hazy about that night).

"Your mother's not breathing well," the nurse said. "We've had to put her on oxygen. We've also called the hospice nurse, and he'll be coming here later. We need him to confer with a doctor about whether we should give her morphine."

Angel and I threw on our jackets and rushed over in the cool evening air. Spring leaves were starting to sprout from the trees, signaling new life.

My mother was prone, her head just slightly raised and her body motionless except for her chest, which heaved with every labored breath. A clear plastic mask covered her mouth and nose. A clear plastic tube snaked from the mask to a portable oxygen tank that stood next to the bed. It was the kind of heavy-duty equipment you might see in a 1950s movie, as if my mother were about to do some undersea exploring to look for the Creature from the Black Lagoon.

Angel and I each took one of her hands and kissed her hello. She blinked and murmured something that we couldn't understand. Over the next couple of hours, her oxygen level improved, getting back to just about normal, but her breathing was still difficult, and the nurses couldn't get a blood pressure reading.

Her eyes were slits, unfocused, and she spoke in confused blurts that we had trouble understanding through the mask.

"Water" was the one word we did understand, and she said it several times. The nurse said it was okay for me to give her a drink, so I stood up and slowly removed her oxygen mask. I extended a cup of ice water and put the straw between her lips. Instead of sucking water into her mouth, she blew into the straw with tiny breaths, sending bubbles into the water. She didn't understand what she was supposed to do. I removed the straw and poured a tiny bit of water into her mouth, nervous that I might drown her.

"Glynn," she said twice. My sister had stopped by earlier that day when we weren't there and had said that my mother stayed asleep the entire time.

"Glynn visited you earlier today, Momma," I gently patted her hand. "She said she had a nice visit, but you didn't quite wake up when she was here. She's at home now and she's doing fine. Angel and I are here with you. And we love you."

She squeezed my hand.

"I love you," she said in a voice that sounded like sleep talking.

The hospice nurse and the nursing home staff concurred that morphine would alleviate her pain and discomfort. But after more than two hours, the prescription still hadn't arrived. As the medication arrived, the hospice nurse said it would be okay if we went home to sleep; she would call if my mother's condition changed.

Surprisingly, I slept better that night than I had earlier in the week.

Sunday, April 10

The next morning, Angel and I arrived at Venerable Hills just before noon. An oxygen mask still covered part of my mother's face, and the head of the bed was still slightly raised. But the 1950s-looking tank had been replaced by a larger, more sophisticated oxygen machine that sat next to the bed. Morphine had set her adrift in what looked like sleep, but her breath was much heavier than a normal sleeping person. Her oxygen level had dropped to an unacceptable level again, and her blood pressure was so low they couldn't get a reading with any device.

A bespectacled doctor arrived and introduced himself. "Normally, it will be the hospice staff that will contact you when the time comes," he said. "It may be someone here at the nursing home, but you'll probably hear from the hospice staff first."

"Okay, thank you." I couldn't even think of any questions. My mind was so blurry that I didn't fully understand what the doctor meant by the phrase "when the time comes." After he left the room, I replayed his words and realized he was talking about her dying. Why didn't they just speak directly and plainly?

Angel and I had brought lunch for ourselves, as well as our much-used deck of cards so we could spend more time by my mother's side. We spoke directly to her as much as possible, although she didn't say a word and didn't open her eyes beyond a tiny slit.

"We're having meatball heroes, Momma," I said. "Remember you and I have had some good food from that place across the street? And Angel and I are playing cards. You and I used to play cards with Pop and Gran, in Kentucky."

I turned back to my lunch and sobbed quietly as I finished eating.

After we finished, Angel got up and stood next to his mother-in-law. "I'm going to comb your hair a little, okay?" he said as he gently neatened the wavy strands with a comb from the dresser drawer. She didn't move or react.

As Angel and I played cards next to the bed, a cheery nurse's aide walked in to take some readings.

"You know, your mother mentioned seeing an angel yesterday," she said with a thick Haitian accent as she checked my mother's pulse. "That means she's a good person. Not everyone gets to see an angel."

Hearing this wowed me. And confused me a bit. My mother didn't believe in heaven or angels. Then I looked at the person sitting next to me, and it made sense.

"You know, *his name* is Angel," I said, motioning to my husband (it's disturbing that in moments like this I was still afraid to refer to him openly as my husband, fearing that if the aide were homophobic, she might mistreat my mother when I wasn't there). "My mother might have been just talking about him because Angel was here yesterday too."

The aide stopped what she was doing. She bent over and clapped her hands, letting out a hearty chortle. "You're kidding me! His name is Angel. Well, that explains it. She must have seen *him*."

A bit later, a nurse arrived to give Eunice her 2 p.m. dose of liquid morphine.

"I'm sorry to bother you, honey," she said to my mother as she bent over to open her mouth and place the dropper inside. "I know you can hear me. This will make you feel better."

I touched my mother's hand again. It was colder than usual. I looked in the closet and found a red-and-white souvenir Brockport blanket decorated with illustrations of local landmarks, including the historic home where she'd worked, the college where she'd studied, and the hospital where I was born and both her husband and father had died. I stretched the blanket over the sheets and took a photo, making sure that "Brockport" was legible.

After a couple of hours, Angel got ready to leave. I began to set up my laptop. I had lots of work to do, and as a freelancer I couldn't take time off or I wouldn't make money. I'd recently bought a portable WiFi device, so I could work from the nursing home and spend more time with my mother.

Angel stood up and walked over to the bed, kissing my mother's cheek and holding her hand as his eyes welled up.

"Goodbye Granny," he said as he kissed her forehead, calling her by the nickname that most people in our family used for her. "Thanks for being such a good mother-in-law. I'm going to miss you. I love you."

My mother lay there, heaving behind the mask.

Like my sister, Angel seemed sure that the end was near. But it was hard for me to accept that she may die soon, for two very different reasons.

First, I dreaded having to say goodbye and lose her. Except for the first four years of my life (which I barely remembered), I'd grown up with her as my only in-house family member. I had no real memories of living with either my father or my sister, so the bond with my mother carried a lot of weight.

Second, I was afraid to get my (or my mother's) hopes up. She wanted to die, and I knew it was best for her. If she were more conscious right now, she'd be thrilled to learn that she was about to depart. But what if she didn't die? What if she were trapped in this semi-conscious state for days, weeks, months? For either of us to feel relief about her finally escaping the pain of life, only to find out that she's going to stick around for months or years more—that would be too depressing for words.

As Angel walked out, I realized my WiFi device wasn't working. "Wait, let me go with you," I called out. "I'll have to get this work done at home. I'll come back in a little while."

"I'll wait for you in the hall," Angel said.

I stood up and packed my computer. "Momma, my computer's not working, so I'm going home for a bit to do some work and I'll come back in just a little while."

I leaned over, held her hand, and kissed her forehead. "I love you Momma. I'll see you in a little bit."

I don't remember saying anything else, but Angel later said that he heard me from the hall, thanking her for being a good mother.

Just before 6:30 p.m., my cell phone rang while I was working at the dining room table. I'd been working for a couple of hours and was on a roll.

"Did you receive a call from the doctor?" a nurse asked.

"No, I haven't received any calls."

"Oh. Someone should have called. I apologize. I'm sorry to inform you that your mother has passed away."

I gave a thumbs-down sign to Angel, who was standing nearby.

I swallowed.

My hands went into the air as soon as I hung up, as if I were trying to grasp a trophy from the sky.

"This is good, this is good," I said, trying to reassure myself through tears as I hugged Angel. "This is a good thing. This is what she wanted. She won't suffer anymore."

As we walked over to Venerable Hills to see my mother for the last time, I pulled out my cell phone to send a text to our friend Richard, who had been planning to visit her after he got out of work.

My mother has died, I wrote. *You don't need to visit today. Let's talk later.*

I'm already here, Richard texted back.

It was a festive day at Venerable Hills when we arrived. A family party was taking place in the library just outside my mother's room, with a man playing guitar and singing in Spanish. The older gentleman being serenaded smiled at me and nodded his head.

And there was Richard, waiting for us in the hallway nearby, wearing dark sunglasses and cloaked in black from head to toe—not because of my mother's passing but because he worked in a trendy store that required extreme fashion statements.

"You look like death," I said as we hugged.

Curtains surrounded my mother's bed. A conversation in Hindi floated from the other half of the room; her roommate had visitors behind those curtains.

We opened the drapes and there was Eunice Chesnut. In the same position as before. But there was no mask. There was no movement. No heaving breaths. The red Brockport blanket was gone, leaving only white sheets. Her hair was still neatly combed, just as Angel had left it earlier.

We stood there for a while and looked at her. I can't remember what we said. Then Angel went out to the hallway to give me some time alone.

I took her hand. It was cool, but no different from what it had been earlier. And it was as soft as always.

Our neighbors' conversations continued from behind the curtain. It would have been a nice courtesy if the nursing home staff had asked them to leave for a while; the visiting family may not have even been aware that someone had just died behind the curtain. Then again, the nursing home may not have realized that the family planned to visit that day, either. Life and death are complicated when you have a roommate.

It was weird to talk to my mother's body with eavesdroppers around. So I spoke under my breath.

"You've done it, Momma! This is what you wanted, and now we don't have to worry about anything anymore. You've had a really amazing life. Thank you for being such a good mother."

I didn't want to leave her yet. But I didn't know what else to say or to do. I had no deep, final words, no issues to resolve. I knew that she'd gone as far as she could at accepting who I was, and that I had gone as far as I could at accepting her way of dealing with that. We'd treated each other as well as we could, and she'd shown much affection and respect for my husband and my relationship. The end result of our years together was pretty good.

But now, it was kind of like when we used to visit my father's grave. There's only so much you can do or say when you're visiting a deceased relative. And there was no monument to a fried-chicken king nearby to provide an alternative topic for conversation.

So I stared at her, touched her hair and face. Lacking anything sufficiently powerful to say, I turned to Hollywood, paraphrasing a couple of lines from the scene in *Mommie Dearest* when Christina is with Joan Crawford's body in the funeral home. (If my mother had suddenly woken up, she would have said, "You're nuts, kid!")

Then I pulled out my cell and took a photo of her. Maybe that sounds weird. But I always liked photographing my mother, and I didn't want our last moments together to fade away. Didn't people in the Victorian era photograph their deceased loved ones too?

I'd often heard people say that family members who've passed look "peaceful." I wouldn't quite say that. My mother just looked still. Motionless. And, like my grandfather when he lay in his casket in the Kentucky funeral home, my mother looked *different*. Her face looked skinnier now, her head at an unnatural angle, and she wore a facial expression that wasn't hers. Her personality wasn't flowing behind that facial façade anymore. But that was okay.

When I got home, I compared the photo I'd just taken of her body to the one I'd taken that same day when she was still alive, with the oxygen mask and the Brockport blanket. Her face and body looked almost exactly the same; not quite her usual presence. Life had already started exiting earlier that day.

Several more weeks passed before I allowed myself to finally turn off my cell phone, which had stayed on, twenty-four hours a day, every day since my mother had arrived in New York City.

Even though I knew her death was normal, natural, and definitely what she wanted, I struggled to put her departure in context.

44. Walking Away

Albany, 1982

Groups of teenagers stood in the parking lot, slamming trunks and hugging parents. The September sky had begun to lose its summer intensity and a cool breeze promised that the leaves would soon change color and cover the grounds, setting a beautiful backdrop for my new life in New York's Capital District.

My mother and I had driven four and a half hours from Brockport so she could drop me off at the State University of New York at Albany. I had chosen that school specifically because it was in a large city that was far from home. Far from the life I needed to leave behind. Albany was too distant for even short weekend visits back home. I'd only go home for major holidays.

This was a fresh start.

I was eager to launch the next phase of my life. My airline fantasies, my imaginary corporate branding, my high school friendships, my mother's permissiveness had all helped me to survive and move forward, even when I felt like an outsider. But it was time to move on. At just seventeen years of age, I somehow realized that life wouldn't be able to progress and evolve if I stayed home. I needed to see if I really would start an airline, or fly around the world, or own a hotel chain, or be a newscaster, or live in a high-rise apartment over-looking downtown Cincinnati, or sleep with businessmen in Columbus. I needed to start my own life.

My mother had her own life, too, of course. She was focused on her work as a historian as well as her volunteer activities, her extensive social life, and even a novel she was writing. She had goals and interests, just like I did. Our paths wouldn't cross as much anymore, but that wasn't necessarily a bad thing. It was a natural progression that meant we were growing. She'd given me the tools and the ability to fend for myself, to *be* myself, even if she didn't fully understand who I was and I didn't quite know yet myself.

It was time to move on.

"Thanks for everything, Mom. I love you."

I gave her a hug and she got into the driver's seat of her metallic blue sedan.

"I love you too, honey," she said, clicking her seat belt and adjusting her large gray sweater. "I'll see you at Thanks-giving. You call me if there's anything you need, and good luck with your classes. Don't forget to study!"

Gravel crunched beneath my feet as I turned and walked toward the dormitory, which was part of a strikingly modern architectural complex designed by Edward Durell Stone, the famed architect responsible for New York City's Lincoln Center. My new life awaited inside that concrete dorm in front of me. I had no idea what it would be like, but I was excited and ready to find out.

For months before our parting of ways in Albany, I'd wondered what it would be like to say goodbye to my mother and be left on my own. I had thought I might cry. But I didn't. The change was necessary. It was good for both of us. It was time for us to start heading our separate ways. I knew she'd always be a part of my life anyway, one way or another.

Which she is.

Previous Publication

An earlier version of "The Last Road Trip" and "The Three Stages of Grief" appeared with the title "Prepare for Departure" in *The Write Launch* (2019)

An earlier version of "Salvation vs. *Star Wars*" appeared with the title "Old Time Religion" in *Stories That Must Be Told* (a Tulip Tree anthology) (2020)

An earlier version of "Feeling Insecure? An Airline Makeover Might Be Just What You Need" appeared with the title "Airline Identity and the Teenage Ego" in *Airplane Reading* (2020)

An earlier version of "Bumps in the Road" appeared in *Belle Ombre* (2020)

An earlier version of "Confessions of a Pre-Teen Airline Addict" appeared in *Away Journal* (2021)

Acknowledgements

I'm a full-time travel writer, not a professional memoirist or purveyor of creative nonfiction. Writing this book was a very different endeavor for me compared to my usual travel articles and hotel reviews. I wrote the essays in this book because I simply *had* to, for emotional and psychological reasons. Crafting these stories helped me to process how I was feeling and move on—and I hope they've also become something that will resonate with other people who've faced similar challenges.

This book would not have been possible without the presence of several people. The first, of course, is my mother, Eunice Clayton Chesnut, who always believed in my abilities and encouraged me to use my imagination and follow my dreams, even if they weren't her own. My husband, Angel Pabón Ramírez, is the other all-important person to thank here. He's always supported me and allowed me to explore my creative passions. His emotional support also helped me to weather the final months of my mother's life, and I can never thank him enough for how kind he was to his mother-in-law.

I'd also like to thank Vine Leaves Press, the fantastic, innovative publisher that decided to take a risk on this book. Thanks to Jessica Bell and Amie McCracken for giving me a chance, and to Melanie Faith for the amazing editing, advice, and support. You should definitely check out more from this publishing company!

My good friend Tammy Joe Smith (who for some reason prefers to be called Mary Beth Anastasio) has also provided invaluable help; she read multiple chapters and provided crucial feedback and encouragement. My good friends Rob Stein, Mark Porter, and Meagan Drillinger also provided ego-boosting when I was feeling down about rejections. And then there's my sister, Glynn Chesnut, who was my valued teammate as we waded through the complexities of my mother's situation.

I've also been lucky to be part of a wonderful writing group that has played a pivotal role in developing this book. Martis Alex, Charlotte Jones, Barbara Weisman, and Roland Scahill—who are all wonderful writers—have provided spectacularly useful input over the past few years that has helped me push my writing to the next level.

I met that talented group of friends while taking memoir writing classes at Gotham Writer's Workshop in New York City, and I must also credit those classes with getting me on the right path as I first started struggling to put words onto my laptop screen. After my mother died, attending those classes reawakened my creativity and helped me to realize that I wasn't done with my own life's work yet; I had a story to share that might entertain and help others.

And then there are the people who made my mother's life happier—including the dedicated healthcare workers at the assisted living and nursing home facilities, as well as my mother's own wonderful group of friends. It's impossible to name them all, but I'll be forever grateful to all those people who provided her with laughter, love, and support. Eunice Chesnut truly appreciated you all, and I do too.

Vine Leaves Press

Enjoyed this book?
Go to *vineleavespress.com* to find more.

CPSIA information can be obtained
at www.ICGtesting.com
Printed in the USA
LVHW031912210622
721725LV00003B/140